TAKING LIBERTIES

ALSO BY ROBERT BOSTON

Why the Religious Right Is Wrong
about Separation of Church and State

The Most Dangerous Man in America?
Pat Robertson and the Rise of the Christian Coalition

Close Encounters with the Religious Right:
Journeys into the Twilight Zone of Religion and Politics

ROBERT BOSTON

TAKING LIBERTIES

WHY
RELIGIOUS FREEDOM
DOESN'T GIVE YOU
THE RIGHT TO TELL
OTHER PEOPLE
WHAT TO DO

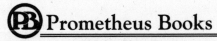

Prometheus Books

59 John Glenn Drive
Amherst, New York 14228

Published 2014 by Prometheus Books

Cover image © Media Bakery
Cover design by Grace M. Conti-Zilsberger

Inquiries should be addressed to
Prometheus Books
59 John Glenn Drive
Amherst, New York 14228
VOICE: 716–691–0133
FAX: 716–691–0137
WWW.PROMETHEUSBOOKS.COM

18 17 16 15 14   5 4 3 2 1

Library of Congress Cataloging-in-Publication Data Pending

ISBN 978-1-61614-911-6 (pbk.)
ISBN 978-1-61614-912-3 (ebook)

Printed in the United States of America

To the memory of my mother, Alice R. Boston

CONTENTS

ACKNOWLEDGMENTS

I'm fortunate because I have been able to spend most of my professional life doing something that means a lot to me: defending the separation of church and state.

I'm doubly fortunate that for over twenty-five years, I've had the privilege to work alongside lots of great people who share the goal of shoring up the church-state wall. There are too many of them to mention by name, but I'd like to single out a few here.

Barry W. Lynn has been executive director of Americans United for Separation of Church and State since 1992. Barry, who is both a minister and an attorney, brings an important perspective to bear in this debate. He's a man of faith who understands why freedom of conscience must be extended to all, believers and nonbelievers, and he intuitively grasps why the government is not the proper agent to promote theology.

Barry drives religious Right leaders crazy. Over the years, I've heard many of them insist that he can't be a "real" minister or that his theology degree must be a fake. I know better. Barry's faith is genuine, and he's comfortable enough with it to believe that it needs no support other than what he and his coreligionists are willing to give it. Barry understands that only a weak religion needs the strut of the state. I suspect that's what really bothers so many people about Barry. Deep down, they envy his uncluttered belief system, which is in contrast to the politicized version they have fashioned. Barry's faith is still about God, worship, and community. The religious Right's is about politicians, ballot boxes, and lobbyists. You see their distress.

Joe Conn was my boss for a quarter of a century. I could not list all that I learned from him. Joe, who served as editor of *Church &*

State (the magazine published by American's United) and ran the media outreach for Americans United, was patient with my learning curve and introduced me to many of the church-state topics I ended up writing about for so long. My life could have turned out very differently if Joe hadn't been such a good boss. I'm glad he was.

The current and former leadership team of Americans United—among them, Ayesha Khan, Maggie Garrett, Beth Corbin, Betsy Pursell, Michael Smoot, Marjorie Spitz Nagrotsky, Aaron Schuham, Richard Katskee, Rebecca Davis-Nord—have been inspiring colleagues and dedicated coworkers. It has been a privilege to labor alongside them in this important cause. I could say that about all the employees of Americans United, past and present. I also deeply appreciate the support (financial and otherwise) of the members of Americans United. We couldn't do this without them—and I mean that literally.

I have also benefitted from the knowledge of many scholars over the years and the research produced by many of the activist groups that work with Americans United. These organizations come in many forms—Jewish, humanist, Christian, and so on. All share the commitment to real religious liberty that the separation of church and state gives us. As the old saying goes, there is strength in numbers, and, through our coalition work, we have learned that, while we may not always agree on points of theology, we definitely agree on the need for a government that respects our right to disagree and doesn't take sides on theological matters.

I'd like to give a special shout-out to the Baptist Joint Committee for Religious Liberty, a group that works to expose the falsehood that Christians don't support the separation of church and state.

Americans United senior litigation counsel, Greg Lipper, gave me some feedback about legal issues. Scott Pichon and Dominic Vallosio, interns in our Field Department, made suggestions that improved the flow of the manuscript. My friend Ivory Madison helped me bring the book into focus during a time when I was still a little fuzzy on what I wanted to say.

On the home front, the support and encouragement of my wife,

Carol, has been absolutely essential. Every day I am reminded that I made the best decision of my life when I asked her to marry me way back in 1991. Our two children, Claire and Paul, bring joy to our lives and remind me of the importance of the work Americans United does so that the next generation will continue to enjoy the benefits of real religious liberty.

I make no claim that the people I have mentioned will agree with everything in this book. The reader may not either. My hope is to foster a discussion about what religious freedom really means in twenty-first-century America. Our experiment in freedom has succeeded well. The only way we can keep it is to continue defending it.

INTRODUCTION

The term *religious freedom* means the right to make decisions about theology for yourself. It's the right to worship God—or not to worship at all—as you see fit. It's the right to share your faith and join in worship with a community of like-minded believers. It's the right to pass that faith on to your children.

That is what religious freedom is. Here is what it is not: It's not the right to tell other people what to do. It's not the right to make decisions for others. It's not the right to use the power of government to impose your theology on anyone else.

There was a time when we had a pretty good understanding of religious freedom in America. That's not surprising, given our nation's history. We took pride in our past. We looked with wonder at our accomplishment: our journey from a nation of Puritans who saw no need to divide religion and government to a vibrant, multifaith society resting on a secular constitution and the separation of church and state.

We had good reason to be proud of that achievement. But for some Americans, that accomplishment, as impressive as it is, has never been enough. They came to believe that our founders' original understanding of religious freedom was faulty, mainly because it put all faiths on an equal plane. To true believers, their religion is the correct one, so it just makes sense that the government should embrace it. (After all, it's true!)

The people who believe this—and there are plenty of them in the United States—would be loath to admit it upfront. Saying you're not for religious freedom or implying that your faith should have more rights than others is akin to saying you don't support the Fourth of July. So these people are attempting to redefine religious freedom. In doing so, they threaten that concept's very existence.

Somewhere along the way, religious liberty has become twisted. Suddenly, it's not about what you can do but what others are doing. Somehow the actions of others are seen as a threat to someone else's religious liberty.

Thus, an employee's decision to use birth control becomes a threat to her boss's religious freedom. An expectation that young children will learn about evolution in a public school endangers the religious freedom of an evolution-denying family in that district. A woman who shows up at a pharmacy and expects the pharmacist to do his job by giving her the medication her doctor has prescribed is threatening the pharmacist's religious freedom. A same-sex couple's decision to get legally married somehow threatens the religious liberty of a person across town who doesn't even know them.

What we're seeing is a deliberate attempt to redefine religious freedom. That concept is being shifted from an individually exercised right to something much different—to something threatened by the independent actions of others. Unless the actions in question involve busting down church doors, thrashing the implements of worship, and threatening the people inside, very little of what one person does affects the religious liberty of another.

Mary's decision to use birth control does nothing to prevent John from attending the church of his choice, praying in whatever manner he sees fit, singing any hymns that he likes, wearing religious garb, or taking part in any other inherently religious activities. If Lisa and Regina decide to get married, Ted across the street is still able to worship as he prefers and attend the church of his choice.

Those who oppose actions like this—the use of birth control and same-sex marriage, to name just two examples—sometimes assert that there is a type of community standard that is threatened by what they perceive to be a creeping form of moral licentiousness.

In fact, there is no such standard when it comes to religious freedom. The only standard that could possibly exist is that religious freedom is a positive value for society. From this point, paths quickly diverge. One man's worship is another's heresy. What one person considers a deep and meaningful religious experience can be rank nonsense to another. There is no such thing as "community faith expression" simply because there is no agreed-upon faith.

Nor does it work to argue that requiring one person to be tolerant of the faith of another somehow breeds a type of complicity. During the recent debate over access to contraceptives, some owners of secular businesses have argued that even tolerating the presence of birth control in an employee healthcare plan is a gross violation of their religious liberty. Bear in mind that these employers are in no way required to pay directly for contraception. Birth control is simply folded into a much larger plan offering an array of healthcare options. Yet we are told that even this is too much, that the mere thought of Jane Employee possibly using birth control is more than Boss Smith's tender sensibilities can bear and is an appalling violation of his religious freedom.

Boss Smith is not required to use birth control, of course. In most cases, Boss Smith isn't even required to pay for it directly because insurance companies are smart enough to know that using birth control is cheaper than having babies, and they adjust rates accordingly. All Boss Smith is required to do is mind his own business. His inability to do this, we are told, amounts to a violation of religious liberty.

There is a rich irony at work here. For years, many of the people who have carped about the actions of others and asserted that someone else's decisions violate their religious liberty have also complained about efforts to enforce the separation of church and state.

Many of these people—activists with the religious Right or adherents of the views held by the US Conference of Catholic Bishops, for example—seek a type of corporate or government-backed expression of religious liberty.

Every time there is a fight over the display of a cross or the Ten Commandments at the seat of government, every time there is a courtroom skirmish over school-sponsored prayer in public institutions, we see this strange idea of corporate religious freedom rearing its head.

Communities, we are told, have religious freedom. And they choose to express it by erecting a cross at city hall. Or they're expressing it with a prayer before a school event that everyone has to participate in or at least listen to.

Efforts to stop such activity by citing the part of the First Amendment that says there shall be no "law respecting an establishment of religion" are usually met with cries that the words have been distorted. The principle is being applied too broadly, we are told. Some even argue, against all available historical evidence, that this provision was meant only to block the erection of an official state church in the United States.

That is a narrow interpretation indeed of what members of the legal profession call the "no-establishment" clause of the First Amendment, and I debunk it in the chapter on history. But if that is indeed the reading many on the religious Right favor, it stands to reason that they would apply the same rather narrow application to the portion of the First Amendment that deals with the "free exercise" of religion. In other words, all that provision is meant to do is to make it illegal, for example, for the government to pass a law banning the practice of Methodism, Lutheranism, Seventh-Day Adventism, and so on.

But that is never what the advocates of corporate religious freedom want. They seek a system whereby the separation of church and state is really just a vehicle for shrinking state power and transferring that power to the church. In other words, this version of religious freedom really does mean the right to tell others what to do, and when government tries to step in to curb that, government is out-of-bounds. After all, no one is setting up a state church, right?

Perhaps not. But nor is the woman who takes a nightly birth-control pill banning the practice of the Catholic faith.

Rather than pretend that our Founding Fathers deliberately bequeathed us a First Amendment with provisions perpetually at war with one another (they weren't that foolish), we would do better to remember the balance inherent in those rights.

Religious freedom is individually expressed as part of the private right of conscience. This freedom is broadly protected and can be curbed only in certain cases. Activities that might endanger the health and safety of others—snake handling, anyone?—are one example. The balance is this: as a corporate right, it fares much more poorly because every time a body of believers attempts to extend its theology outward by harnessing government power, it infringes on the rights of others.

The problem seems to stem from the belief some bosses have that they can control their employees' lives outside the workplace. In fact, American culture and traditions value the opposite: the right to self-determination. Many major religions express this concept (i.e., the right to be the boss of yourself) in lofty terms. Baptists hew to what they call the "priesthood of the believer," the idea that every man and woman is free to interpret the scriptures as guided by conscience. Colonial-era religious-liberty pioneer Roger Williams called it "soul liberty."

Of course, most of us have a boss at some point in our lives. And he or she really is the boss of us, in some areas. At work, the boss hands out the assignments and divvies up the duties. You might not like the task you get, but if you don't get to it, you'll join the unemployment line.

But that's work. Inside you, in what some might call your spirit, in what a Supreme Court justice once eloquently referred to as the "inviolable citadel of the individual heart and mind,"[1] no one is the boss of you but you.

You decide where to worship or whether to worship at all. You decide whom to worship with. You decide how often to worship. You decide what god (or gods) to worship. And, if you're among an increasing number of Americans, you decide what worship means.

If dogma's not your thing, you can be "spiritual but not religious." You decide what words like *god*, *spirit*, and *prayer* mean.

There was a time when it would have been shocking to assume this right. Many people who tried it have been killed. To worship outside the confines of a favored church was to tempt the inquisitor and his rack. In short, it was itself an affront to God.

Those days are long gone, at least in America. But that does not mean some do not pine for them still. As someone who has spent a quarter of a century defending the separation of church and state, I've concluded that there are those among us who think our founders made a mistake when they crafted the First Amendment.

The people who believe this aren't willing to admit it publicly. As I said, assailing the concept of religious freedom wins you no friends. So these people don't say this in words, but their actions speak it for them.

Too much freedom, we are told, is a dangerous thing. Given too many choices, some will choose wrongly. Those who have chosen wrongly—that is, joined a religion that fundamentalists don't like—have put their immortal souls in jeopardy. To the religious zealots among us, one of the jobs of government is to pave the one true path to heaven, not fill it with off ramps.

Thus, to the fundamentalists and ultraorthodox among us, the actions of others become an assault on their religious freedom because these others force the fundamentalists to stand by helplessly as another soul goes wandering down the wrong road.

The problem with this is obvious: everyone thinks they're on the right road and that other folks are misguided. One person's highway to heaven is another person's road to hell, and vice versa. As long as people look at religious freedom this way, as some sort of hedge against people making poor decisions about faith and philosophies, as long as people persist in believing that someone else's "wrong" decision about faith or morals impacts them, we won't have peace. We are fated to endure an endless series of culture wars.

But it does not have to be this way. We could begin by dedicating ourselves anew to the original spirit of religious freedom, which is, quite simply, your right to believe as you will and to worship (or not) as you will—also, most importantly, it is to accept that the only person you get to subject to religious control is yourself.

Thomas Jefferson said it best: "The legitimate powers of government extend to such acts only as are injurious to others. But it does me no injury for my neighbour to say there are twenty gods, or no god. It neither picks my pocket nor breaks my leg."[2]

One of our problems today is that too many people are convinced that what their neighbors believe about religion—and, more importantly, how that plays out in daily life—is picking pockets and breaking legs with abandon.

This book is designed to replace the stolen wallets and straighten out the legs. It will tell you to believe what you will, and it even celebrates that right. But remember, you don't have the right to tell others what to do.

In this book, I also argue, without apology, for the idea that the public interest and the public good sometimes must override an asserted claim of religious freedom. The fact is, people make all kinds of claims about religious freedom. An attempt to honor them all would grind society to a halt.

As I was writing this book, a man in Nevada attempted to claim that he had a religious-freedom right not to pay federal income tax. This did not go over well. A federal court ruled against him, declaring, "Courts have routinely held that the federal government's taxing power cannot be resisted on the basis of a religious objection, for the interest in maintaining an efficient and orderly taxation system is compelling justification for burdens on religious freedom."[3]

In other words, the public good, represented by the need to collect taxes, trumps a religious-liberty claim.

As I was writing this book, a state judge in Wisconsin rejected a claim brought by an Amish farmer that his religious beliefs shielded him from being brought into court for selling unpasteurized milk.

The farmer argued that his religious beliefs forbade him from inter-
acting with the court system at all. His defense failed, as there is
a public good in maintaining an effective court system that can
resolve legal and civil matters, that valid public interest must trump
religious freedom claims. (The farmer's case went before a jury, and
he was acquitted.)[4]

*   *   *

Now for a few words about terminology. The conservative religious
movements that I discuss in this book consist primarily of two
camps: (1) theologically and politically conservative Protestants
and (2) the hierarchy of the Roman Catholic Church.

People often call the former camp the "religious Right." It's not
a perfect term. Some conservatives are quite religious yet support
church-state separation and would rankle at the thought of being
lumped in with the religious Right.

Likewise, many individual Catholics break with their bishops on
issues of social policy. Indeed, when it comes to something like birth
control, the numbers are truly staggering. The vast majority of
American Catholics simply aren't listening to the bishops on this issue.
Most Catholic women will, at some point in their lives, use artificial
forms of birth control—just as most non-Catholic women will.

The chiefly Protestant religious Right and the Catholic hierarchy don't agree on every issue I talk about in this book. While
they're in accord on opposition to legal abortion, same-sex marriage, and, increasingly, access to birth control, they don't see eye
to eye on an issue like the teaching of evolution in public schools.
The Catholic Church's official line is that evolution should be
taught as long as it isn't done in such a way as to suggest that
God had no role to play in the creation of the universe. In addition,
the mostly Protestant religious Right, which for years has been an
appendage of the Republican Party, often takes stands on nonsocial
issues (guns, immigration, the economy, etc.) that mirror those held

by the institutional GOP. The bishops often break with the right wing on these issues. (But, as many bishops are fond of reminding Americans every time there is an election, issues like abortion and marriage trump all the others.)

It isn't always practical to separate these camps in every case I discuss in these pages, especially because I'm dealing solely with social issues here. Thus, sometimes I use phrases like "the religious Right" and "religious conservatives" to include the bishops, and sometimes that term will not include them. I trust the context will make this clear.

I'm also aware that some analysts believe that the religious Right as a political movement is on the skids. I might put more stock in such claims if I hadn't been hearing them for the past twenty-five years.

Clearly, some long-term trends do not bode well for the religious Right. Elsewhere in this book, I discuss the shifting polling data on the issue of same-sex marriage. Polls consistently show that younger Americans don't object to marriage equality. The tide is turning, and this issue is likely to lose some of its potency in the years to come.

But those same polls also show a closer divide over other "culture war" issues such as legal abortion, the role of religion in public life, religion in public schools, and even the topic of this book—that is, the parameters of religious freedom. These issues will provide religious Right groups with enough fodder for the foreseeable future.

The religious Right also remains very powerful in the Republican Party, an institution that, despite what some would have you believe, isn't quite dead yet. Far Right Republicans control or have substantial influence in the legislatures of a number of states (twenty-four, by some counts), many of them swept into power in 2010.

In those states, they are pushing an extremely conservative social agenda that includes measures designed to ban nearly all abortions, reintroduce formal prayer into public schools, and curb the teaching of evolution.

As I was writing this book, many political pundits were asserting that the Republican Party would have to moderate on the issue of same-sex marriage to remain viable. I see no evidence of this. Not only did GOP leaders not do that, they did the opposite and reaffirmed their opposition to marriage equality—mainly to keep the religious Right happy.

Despite what some political prognosticators believe, the election of Barack Obama in 2008 and his reelection in 2012 did little to slow down the religious Right. Certainly, the results of the elections disappointed these groups, but these organizations were also energized by their opposition of Obama. In the 2010 midterm election, just two years after some pundits said Obama had crushed the right wing and permanently realigned American politics, the Far Right came roaring back, pumped up by an infusion of energy from Tea Party groups, a movement that shares much in common with the religious Right. (I am aware that not all Tea Party supporters agree with the religious Right's social agenda; some are secular conservatives whose main issues are things like taxes and regulation. Those people are the minority. Polls show that the vast majority of self-identified Tea Party backers agree with the religious Right on social issues, and, at a string of national conferences held by religious Right groups that I attended in 2010–2012, the efforts to combine the two movements into one large, right-wing phalanx were obvious.)

I am critical of the religious Right in this book, but I hope that readers will not perceive anything within these pages as an attack on religion. That is not my intention. Through my work at Americans United for Separation of Church and State, I have often labored alongside many deeply devout people who understand that church-state separation is a great boon to faith. The rather vicious and disheartening attacks on the church-state wall tend to come from a narrow segment of the American religious community (which most people call the religious Right) and don't represent mainstream American religious opinion.

Nor do most American believers seek to impose their faith on others. Most people of faith are happy to live and let live when it comes to matters of religion. They would be happy to discuss their beliefs with anyone who asks, but they don't seek to impose that faith on others through the power of government.

Religion is not the problem. Fundamentalist religion that seeks to merge with political power and impose its dogma on the unwilling is the problem.

I have no beef with people of faith. I have a big one with anyone who considers the raw power of government an appropriate vehicle for evangelism.

1

HISTORY

A lot of countries don't have religious freedom. In many nations, the government presumes to tell people what to believe and how to behave when it comes to religion. Saudi Arabia, where faiths outside Wahhabi Islam are illegal, is an extreme example.

But even some generally tolerant Western nations regulate (or attempt to regulate) the religious behaviors of their citizens. The practice of Scientology is illegal in Germany, and some states there still attempt to place restrictions on the faith of Jehovah's Witnesses.

The United States took a different path. Why?

The short answer is that we have religious freedom in America because there was a time when we didn't, and we learned from that. This period of restrictions on religious liberty was not an abstraction to key founders. They lived through it; they observed it firsthand. Having seen the results of colonies where there was no meaningful religious freedom, they sought to protect its practice.

I have discussed the history of this period in one of my previous books, *Why the Religious Right Is Wrong about Separation of Church and State*.[1] It's not my intention to revisit all of that again here, but it is important to take a quick look at the development of religious freedom in the United States. As is often the case, a glance backward tells us how we got to where we are.

This is important because the use (or misuse) of history is fundamental to the strategy of those who would redefine religious freedom. They have constructed a narrative—one that does not necessarily jibe with the facts—to buttress this redefinition.

One of the things they have sought to do is decouple religious freedom from the concept of the separation of church and state. These two concepts—religious liberty and church-state separation—have been portrayed as enemies and have been made to fight. The implication here is that the American people will have to choose: Do they want separation or religious liberty? We are told that our nation can't have both.

Actually, we can. In fact, we have. Indeed, we must. Religious freedom is not the enemy of separation of church and state. These two concepts are partners. More than that, they're like mutualistic organisms. They need one another to survive. The founders knew this; that's why the First Amendment says what it does.

Prior to the founders, early religious-liberty pioneers also understood this. Roger Williams, an iconoclastic minister and the founder of Rhode Island, challenged the Puritan establishment of Massachusetts with a bold demand for "soul liberty." Williams maintained that the state had no business dictating orthodoxy to anyone. His preferred method of making certain that the government did not do this was the separation of church and state.

Williams's separation was not merely the end of established churches, although he certainly favored that. He insisted that the government had no right to compel anyone to recite a religious oath, and he blasted attempts by the state to define which religions were pleasing to God. Such attempts inevitably led to persecution, Williams maintained. And compulsory religion, he argued, "stinks in the nostrils of God."[2]

Williams's ideas were heretical at the time. Indeed, Massachusetts's ruling Puritans found him tiresome and had plans to forcibly ship him back to England. Williams escaped and fled into the wilderness. He purchased (rather than simply seized) land from the natives and founded his own colony—Providence.

Meaningful religious liberty, Williams believed, encompasses the right to be wrong from someone else's perspective. And this wasn't just talk on his part; Williams put it into practice. Williams was not fond of Quakers and found their theology strange. Yet Quakers worshipped unmolested in Providence. If Quakers were wrong, Williams believed, God would have an opportunity to explain that to them at some point. It was not the magistrate's job.

In a famous metaphor, Williams spoke of a "wall of separation between the garden of the church and the wilderness of the world."[3] The phrase is interesting because it anticipates something Thomas Jefferson said many years later—although there is no evidence that Jefferson knew of it.

We get the impression here that Williams is advocating for the purity of the church in the face of state encroachments. Randall Balmer, a highly respected scholar of American religion, has pointed out that the word *wilderness* had great meaning for the men and women of Williams's day. It's likely Williams chose it with great care.

Balmer notes that the Puritans viewed the wilderness as a frightening place, untamed and full of dangers. To mix the church with the wilderness, then, was a great threat to the church. Williams's separation was in no way designed to lessen the power or purity of belief. In fact, this wall was a protector, not a destroyer.[4]

As European settlements grew along the East Coast, colonies adopted various rules relating to religious freedom. Some had established churches, while others were more liberal in their attitude.

In those colonies with official state churches, dissenting clergy members were the first to raise the argument for separation of church and state. A distance between the two institutions, they argued, was the only way to ensure freedom of belief for all.

Some pastors framed their argument in explicitly theological terms. Official establishments, they argued, served the interests of neither church nor state.

Isaac Backus, a colonial-era Baptist preacher in New England, argued the former, asserting, "Religious matters are to be separated from the jurisdiction of the state, not because they are beneath the interests of the state but, quite to the contrary, because they are too high and holy and thus are beyond the competence of the state."[5]

John Leland, an especially fiery Baptist cleric, worked his entire life to end established churches and any government interference in soul liberty. Leland argued that mere toleration was not enough. The government had to get out of the religion business entirely.

"The liberty I contend for is more than toleration," Leland wrote in 1820. "The very idea of toleration is despicable; it supposes that some have a pre-eminence above the rest to grant indulgence; whereas all should be equally free, Jews, Turks [Muslims], Pagans and Christians. Test oaths and established creeds should be avoided as the worst of evils."[6]

Leland holds an unusual distinction in American political history: he helped end state-established churches in three states. He is perhaps best known for providing a theological voice to the efforts of Thomas Jefferson and James Madison to free Virginia from the Anglican establishment. Less well-known are his efforts in his home state of Massachusetts. The Bay State was the last to surrender its established church, finally cutting it loose in 1833. Leland, who died in 1841, helped lead the charge for disestablishment. While doing that, he found time to make cross border raids into Connecticut, where he assisted pro-disestablishment forces there.

Although Leland's theology was conservative, he had no problem embracing Jefferson, whose religious views were notoriously unorthodox. Leland was influenced by Jefferson, who combined elements of Deism and European Enlightenment with a Christianity stripped of miracles and mysticism, thus creating his own idiosyncratic brew. In 1791, Leland called for the right of "every man to speak freely without fear—maintain the principles that he believes—worship according to his own faith, either one God, three Gods, no God, or twenty Gods."[7] Ten years earlier, in his *Notes on the State of Virginia*, Jefferson observed something similar, "It does me no injury for my neighbor to say there are twenty gods or no God. It neither picks my pocket nor breaks my leg."[8]

Jefferson and Leland didn't agree on theology. But they remained close and worked together to promote the separation of church and state because both understood that true freedom could not exist when the government imposed religion on its citizens.

Remember, religious persecution was not an abstraction to people like Jefferson and Leland. They saw it. They lived it. Jefferson's partner and protégé, James Madison, became a powerful advocate for church-state separation after seeing "well-meaning men" in jail because they dared to preach their Baptist doctrines on the street. Madison was especially incensed that so many members of the established clergy in Virginia backed this type of persecution.

Religious freedom, then, to many people of the founding period, chiefly meant the right to worship as one saw fit. Despite the actions of people like Jefferson, Madison, and their allies in the dissenting clergy, it was by no means clear that this right would be secure everywhere. It had to be fought for in some states. In Virginia, Jefferson and Madison worked together to end the established Anglican church and pass a law giving all residents the right to worship as they saw fit.

The Virginia Statute for Religious Freedom, drafted by Jefferson, was a pioneering piece of legislation when it was enacted in 1786. Many historians believe it influenced Madison so strongly that he took its values with him when he played a key role in authoring the First Amendment.

But, for the time being, it remained only a Virginia law. The level of religious liberty in other states varied. The situation was so unsettled that members of minority groups felt uncertain about their status.

In 1790, the leadership of Touro Synagogue in Newport, Rhode Island, wrote to President George Washington to express its concerns over the rights of Jews in the new nation. The leaders noted that they had been "Deprived as we heretofore have been of the invaluable rights of free Citizens,"[9] and they expressed their desire for a nation free from bigotry and persecution.

Washington's eloquent reply is a classic of religious liberty. He assured the synagogue's leaders of their rightful place in America, writing, "The citizens of the United States of America have a right to applaud themselves for having given to mankind examples of an enlarged and liberal policy—a policy worthy of imitation. All possess alike liberty of conscience and immunities of citizenship. It is now no more that toleration is spoken of as if it were the indulgence of one class of people that another enjoyed the exercise of their inherent natural rights, for, happily, the Government of the United States, which gives to bigotry no sanction, to persecution no assistance, requires only that they who live under its protection should demean themselves as good citizens in giving it on all occasions their effectual support."[10]

Powerful words. But at the time Washington penned them, they were not backed by anything official. The Bill of Rights, with its First Amendment guarantee of religious freedom, had yet to be added to the Constitution. In some states, Jews did face persecution. Indeed, some states even barred them from holding public office. And in the states that retained established churches, Jews, along with everyone else, had to support these official religious institutions even though they did not belong to those churches or even believe in their doctrines.

Much of this history is disputed by the religious Right. It's disputed in much the same way that some people dispute the theory of evolution. Through a selective culling of history, backed by a campaign of distortions and outright lies, they have created an alternate "history."

But it's not history, just as "creation science" isn't science. I'm old-fashioned enough to believe that if something didn't actually happen, it doesn't qualify as history. It's something else: it's a myth, a legend, a comforting (for some) story, even. Not history. History is the stuff that actually happened, not the stuff you wish had happened.

The "Christian nation" didn't happen. If it had, we would see evidence of it. First and foremost, we would see it in our Constitution. It is not there. That document contains no references in the body of the text to Christianity, Jesus Christ, or God, for that matter.

There are just two references to religion in the Constitution. One is in the First Amendment, which we've already touched on. The other is found at the end of Article VI, which states that there shall be "no religious test" for public office. This is an odd provision to put into a constitution of a Christian nation, is it not? Language that guarantees everyone—Christian and non-Christian—the right to hold federal office hardly establishes a Christian nation. It rather cuts the other way.

Furthermore, ultraconservative Protestant groups in the wake of the Civil War tried repeatedly to add a Christian-nation amendment to the Constitution.[11] Why would they have wanted to do that if the Constitution already acknowledged Christianity?

The answer is because the Constitution didn't do that, and the extremely conservative ministers of that time, a kind of prototypical religious Right, knew that. They considered it a flaw, and they wanted to see it corrected.

Interestingly, the Christian-nation concept first took off during the Civil War, when minsters in the North, distraught over the Union Army's early losses, began asserting that the battlefield reverses were God's punishment on the nation for spurning him in the Constitution.

Later, as the North turned the tide and it became obvious that the South was going to lose, these same ministers changed their tune and began claiming that God favored the North because it was more spiritually upright than the South. Their argument suddenly shifted, and they began asserting that the framers of the Constitution had meant to add recognition of Christianity to the Constitution but had failed for some unknown reason, so it was up to these ministers to complete that task. Amazingly, they argued with a straight face that our secular Constitution somehow perpetuated a Christian order anyway and that adding a Christian-nation amendment would merely codify this.

In the modern era, an entire cottage industry has sprung up in religious Right circles, offering this phony history to fundamentalist throngs. I call it "historical creationism," and, indeed, the parallels between ersatz history and junk science draped in clerical vestments are startling.

Neither stands up to examination well. Real scientists have debunked creationism (including its younger, hipper cousin, "intelligent design") more times than I care to count. Similarly, actual historians and other scholars have let loose on the Christian-nation canard so many times that it should have ended up in the trash heap a long time ago. It survives because its main support system is the will to believe, not real research.

David Barton, a Texas man who is not a historian, has for many years made a living peddling the Christian-nation myth to eager audiences. His main claims are that Thomas Jefferson and other founders didn't really support church-state separation and that the United States was founded to be an officially Christian nation.

In 2012, Barton's carefully constructed cardboard village of phony history came crashing down when a number of Christian scholars, led by Warren Throckmorton and Michael Coulter at Grove City College in Pennsylvania, finally decided they'd had enough and dissected his tall tales bit by bit.[12]

Others had done it before Throckmorton and Coulter (a researcher named Chris Rodda has been especially active), but the Throckmorton/Coulter broadside, which, among other things, debunked Barton's fallacious claims about Jefferson's personal religious views, stung Barton especially hard because these guys were hardly flaming liberals. Until then, Barton's typical response to his critics had been exactly that: it's all political.

Maybe it's not all political. Maybe it really is about history. Maybe it's something as simple as being offended by bad history or something that's not really history after all.

Obviously, history is open to interpretation. Scholars look at events from the past, marshal evidence, and present conclusions. If you want to upset the conventional wisdom concerning a historical incident, by all means, have at it. But you must present some evidence; you must make the case.

You must also understand that history is a record of things that happened. As I've pointed out, events that never happened are not history. Barton argues that the United States was deliberately founded to be a Christian nation, but that never happened. What he promotes is not history; it is something else.

As of this writing, Barton continues to hang on. A book he wrote purporting to debunk lies about Jefferson was so full of errors that the publisher took the rare step of withdrawing it from circulation. (A flavor for this book can perhaps be gained by its main argument: Jefferson, the man who rejected the divinity of Jesus, the miracles of the New Testament, and the resurrection, was really an evangelical Christian. It got worse from there.)

The Christian-nation crowd is famous for taking a kernel of truth and turning it into an entire bag of buttery popcorn. One thing they point out is that the First Amendment didn't apply to states when it was adopted.

This is hardly a news flash. The First Amendment begins with the word *Congress*, after all. So what happened? It wasn't until well into the nineteenth century, with the adoption of the Fourteenth Amendment in the post–Civil War period, that portions of the Bill of Rights came to be binding on the states. Incredibly, this concept (known as *incorporation*) was not embraced by the Supreme Court until the 1920s.

Another favorite of the religious Right is to assert that separation of church and state is a myth or a concept conjured up by liberal judges in the modern era. They often point to a famous letter Thomas Jefferson wrote in 1802 in which he invoked the metaphor of the First Amendment, creating "a wall of separation between church and state."[13]

Playing a game of historical gotcha, religious Right activists argue that Jefferson didn't write the First Amendment and was, in fact, in France when it was adopted. The implication is that this makes him somehow unfit to comment on the First Amendment— even though the Virginia Statute for Religious Freedom, which

Jefferson did write, clearly influenced the First Amendment's religion provisions.

The problem with this argument is that we do not have separation of church and state because Jefferson once said we did in a letter. We have it because the scope and effect of the First Amendment is to separate church and state. Jefferson's letter is an interesting and important commentary on the First Amendment. (And, I would add, even though he was in France during the deliberations over the Bill of Rights, he was alive and active at the time of the founding— something no modern-day commentator can claim.) Yet the separation of church and state does not spring from Jefferson's letter to the Danbury Baptists. It springs from the First Amendment.

Creationists often seem to think they can find a smoking-gun quote that would cause the theory of evolution to collapse. Some of them have taken to asserting that Charles Darwin renounced the theory on his deathbed. The story isn't true, but even if it were, it would not undermine evolutionary theory. The theory of evolution isn't proven true because of one book Darwin wrote. It is proven by the confluence of evidence that has been identified since then.

The historical creationists of the religious Right make the same mistake with church-state separation. They think all they have to do is debunk one letter or identify one quote from another founder that challenges the thinking of Jefferson and Madison, and then they will have proven that separation of church and state is a lie.

It's not so. The development of the separation of church and state in America rests not on one letter, one comment, or even one Supreme Court ruling. A confluence of evidence proves that a division between religion and government was the founders' intent.

Did this policy of separation, which had never been implemented anywhere in the world previously, go off perfectly well without a hitch? Of course not. The history of religious freedom in America is not as smooth as some would think today. The adoption of the First Amendment was a significant milestone, but it did little to thwart cultural assumptions that the United States was, unofficially, at least, a Protestant nation. Indeed, Christian practices (and by *Christian*, I mean here generically Protestant) infiltrated many laws well into the twentieth century.

Old habits die hard. The vision of people like Roger Williams and, later, Jefferson and Madison was for a nation of many faiths, where people lived in peace side by side—but it is taking some time to get there. Some visions are more far-reaching than others. Jefferson frequently spoke of the religious-liberty rights of not just Christians and Jews but even "infidels" and "pagans." There are still people today who resist that idea.

This full vision of Williams, Leland, Jefferson, and Madison was not embraced in America until well into the modern era. For many years, a type of begrudging tolerance was the norm. Religious minorities were welcome in America, and there were no legal proscriptions against their worship—but they had to remember their place. The outbreak of tensions between Roman Catholics and Protestants in the latter half of the nineteenth century tested this arrangement. (Catholic parents were the first to challenge official prayer and Bible reading in public schools because the practices were Protestant in nature and were often little more than an obnoxious daily reminder to the Catholics of the second-class status of their faith. See more on this in the chapter on education.)

The spread of Mormonism in the nineteenth century was another test. Although the Mormons, who, at the time, practiced polygamy, lost every case they brought to the Supreme Court, their insistence on being heard in court forced the nation to confront the question of what the "free exercise" of religion really meant.

The answer was that free exercise granted no right to violate the law. In one of the first Mormon cases, *Reynolds v. United States*, the Supreme Court in 1879 basically said that you have the right to believe whatever you want but that your ability to act on those beliefs may be subject to certain restrictions.

This would seem an obvious point. Yet it was the guiding principle of much religious-freedom law for a long time. How did we get from there to the point where we are today—where a secular employer argues that his religious-freedom rights are violated because his employees choose to use birth control?

The short answer is that courts began to shift in the modern era. The religious Right is loath to admit this, but around the same time the courts were adopting a more expansive vision of what constitutes an "establishment" of religion, they were also more broadly interpreting free-exercise rights.

Thus, by 1972, the Amish had won the right to pull their children out of school after the eighth grade, even though most states by then had laws requiring children to be educated much longer.[14]

But even that doesn't tell the entire story. The missing piece of the puzzle is that religious groups over the years became very adept at lobbying. They learned how to turn up the pressure and get what they wanted—that is, at least the lobbies representing the powerful and large religions did.

Unlike lobbyists for secular entities and corporations, church lobbyists don't waltz into the offices of members of Congress and start throwing wads of cash around. They don't have to. In a society as religious as the United States, it's merely enough for these lobbies to be religious and to properly frame an argument.

Some learned to play the victim when they failed to get what they wanted. Recent debates over healthcare and access to contraceptives have been marked by allegations of anti-Catholicism. The implication is that any legislator who fails to give in to the demands of the US Conference of Catholic Bishops, any lawmaker who happens to believe that the health needs of average people trumps the asserted conscience rights of a church, is anti-Catholic.

We've come to the point where even a refusal to extend tax support to the schools and other projects run by churches is labeled a form of bias. The Catholic bishops have—several times—argued that the refusal to award state support to their private-school network is motivated by anti-Catholicism, as if there could be no other motive (such as believing that the public-school system should get the money because it serves 90 percent of our children, or that church projects ought, by right, to be funded with church money).

In making such claims, religious leaders conveniently fail to raise certain relevant facts. That they are tax exempt is perhaps the most salient. Tax exemption is a very desirable benefit. In America, it is extended to religious groups by mere dint of their existence; there's no need to fill out a lot of paperwork like secular nonprofits must do. (See more on this in the chapter on persecution.)

Once given, tax exemption is rarely revoked, at least for religious groups, anyway. Only the most overt and obnoxious forms of fraud will incur an examination from the Internal Revenue Service. If you doubt this, merely consider the panoply of television evangelists who prowl the airwaves, flying from coast to coast on tax-free jumbo jets as they shuttle from one tax-exempt mansion to another, often appointing family members as instant ministers so they too can get in on the largess.

Or look at the political activities. Many churches and ministries openly flout federal laws that bar tax-exempt groups from intervening in political races between candidates. They simply ignore it. The IRS knows about it—yet it does nothing. Secular nonprofits that fail to comply, however, will soon find that their tax-exempt status is a memory. (There's more on this in the chapter on politics.)

The law has come to privilege religion in many ways. In most cases, this isn't because the courts have interpreted the free exercise of religion to demand it; it's because church lobbyists and pressure groups have launched successful lobbying campaigns.

In some states, secular daycare centers are closely regulated and monitored by government agencies to ensure the health and safety of the children who attend them. Religious daycare centers are wholly exempt—they aren't even required to meet basic codes for safety (and often this has the predictable disastrous results).[15]

No Supreme Court ruling says that church-run daycare centers must, under the First Amendment, be free from all government oversight and even minimal regulation. In fact, the Supreme Court would be extremely unlikely to say this. Given the obvious compelling government interest in ensuring that infants and toddlers are in safe environments, the argument that a church-sponsored daycare center had a right under the Constitution to be absolutely free of all forms of monitoring would be very difficult to make in court successfully.

So why in some states are church-run daycare centers subjected to no oversight? It's not because courts have mandated it as a necessary thing under religious freedom; it's because religious lobbyists won that concession on behalf of church-run daycare centers by trolling the halls at the state capital. And, so far, no group has mounted an effective counterstrategy to change the law.

In other words, religious groups won an exception from the law everyone else must follow. To ensure the health and safety of little children, legislators in some states passed a law limiting the number of children daycare centers could care for and subjecting said daycare centers to inspections. Religious groups did not want to comply with this law, so they lobbied for and won an exception.

Over time, these groups came to believe that their legislatively granted exemptions were a constitutional right. Or they made that argument in court, hoping to make that the case. Or they simply asserted it to the public through the media.

The situation has deteriorated to the point where people are now seriously arguing that their religious beliefs give them the right not to do jobs they were hired to do.

Pharmacists across the country have refused to fill prescriptions for birth-control or Plan B pills because they say they have a religious freedom right not to. For a time, Muslim taxi drivers at the Minneapolis–Saint Paul airport were refusing to transport anyone carrying bottles of alcohol, even though the bottles were sealed. Wedding planners, florists, bakers, and the owners of bed-and-breakfasts are refusing service to same-sex couples. Again the cry is raised of "religious freedom."

No one is asking the obvious question: Does the private choice of another person prevent you from attending the house of worship of your choice? Further, does it stop you from joining your coreligionists for prayer and worship? Does it require you to bow before an alien god?

The pharmacists, taxi drivers, B&B owners, and so on concede that it does not. But they go on to argue that they don't wish to be complicit in another's sin. Putting aside the question of whether the government has any obligation to (or is even legally permitted to) recognize what qualifies as "sin," the standard being proposed for adoption here is dangerously vague and loose.

"Sin" is a notoriously slippery concept. One person's sin can easily be another's hobby or harmless preference. Examples include dancing, reading steamy novels, and wearing tight clothing.

A society where a self-asserted claim to religious liberty trumps every other right quickly becomes unworkable. What's to stop a Muslim store clerk from refusing to ring up your bacon? Don't laugh—it has happened. Why not allow the clerk in the bookstore to refuse to tell you where the sex manuals are kept because you're not married? What prevents the woman at the register from turning you away because your skirt is just a little too short?

Some might say these are minor inconveniences. After all, there will always be another store, another clerk, another skirt. Perhaps so.

But what happens when it's three o'clock in the morning and the only clerk at the only twenty-four-hour pharmacy in town won't give a victim of sexual assault a pack of Plan B pills sitting six inches away from his hand? What happens when a woman with a problem pregnancy can't get a taxi driver to take her to an abortion clinic? What happens when an entire family is turned away from a hotel because the owner doesn't think much of their religion?

More to the point, in such a society, what's to stop grotesque invasions of privacy under the guise of protecting someone else's freedom of religion? The owners of secular businesses who don't want to include birth control in healthcare plans assume that their employees will use it to avoid pregnancy. Indeed, most probably will.

But some will use birth-control pills to shrink ovarian cysts. Some will use them to treat endometriosis. Some will even use them for cases of acne.

Why should an employer's so-called right to refuse to include birth control in a healthcare plan—a regulation that in no way prevents the employer from attending religious services, praying, or reading the religious texts of choice, or even taking part in numerous other forms of religious expression—override the employee's right to get and use possibly lifesaving medicine? If these rights are deemed to be in conflict, it would seem the claim for medicine is stronger. After all, the inability to get this medicine can, in some cases, have extremely serious consequences. (Untreated endometriosis can lead to chronic pain, cysts, infertility, and even cancer.)

Another option is to require women who want birth-control pills for reasons that aren't related to, well, the control of births to submit a doctor's note to their employers. How patronizing is that? How much private medical information does that require the employee to divulge? If we accept the proposition that one person must jump through a series of absurd, demeaning hoops so that another person may fully exercise his or her religious liberty, then something is seriously amiss.

The line is drawn exactly where? The Church of Scientology has a well-known animus toward the psychiatric profession. If your boss down at the lumber mill is a Scientologist, can he refuse to cover any employee's visits to a counselor for any reason? Can he deny couples access to a marriage counselor and cut off paying for drugs that treat things like depression, attention deficit disorder, or schizophrenia?

Can a factory owner who happens to be a Jehovah's Witness refuse to put surgical procedures into healthcare plans because they involve blood transfusions? More to the point, can a fundamentalist Christian who owns a chain of home-improvement stores announce that the requirement to provide a healthcare plan to employees is, in itself, unconstitutional because no one needs to see a doctor? You just need to pray, and Jesus will heal you.

What about a New Age boss who argues that all healing comes from herbs, vitamins, and crystals, and that's all that will be covered?

Can these business owners do these things? Why not? How are they different than what Catholic opponents of birth control have asserted? Once a broad right to religious freedom has been asserted—so broad that it gives the boss the right to control the private decisions of others—no distinctions can be made between religions. All must be treated equally.

Here's a simpler solution: you have no control over others. What medications I use and what I use them for aren't your business. My need or choice to swallow pill A or get treatment B doesn't stop you from worshipping, praying, or relating to God in whatever way you see fit.

If you feel these actions endanger my soul, feel free to tell me that. But that's it. You don't have a say over me or my soul. Having examined the facts, we are capable of making our own decisions about our souls—where they will end up, how they might get there, and even if they exist.

Williams, Leland, Jefferson, and Madison understood this. At a time when real religious liberty was a rarity in the world, they grasped an important fact: religious liberty is, first and foremost, the right to make decisions *for yourself.*

This may seem utterly noncontroversial today. It is only because a generation of pioneers paved the way to make it so. Prior to the founders, just about every government in human history assumed it had the right (and the duty) to "help" subjects refrain from making theological mistakes, to prevent them from straying into error.

There were at least two problems with this: First, different nations and leaders had various ideas as to what constituted theological "error." Catholic France and Protestant England never could quite see eye to eye on this matter. Nor could Orthodox Russia. Or Muslim Turkey, for that matter. You get the idea.

Second, people continued to make it abundantly clear that they did not need, nor did they want, this state-sponsored "help" in matters of religion. They even considered it offensive. And annoying. Even dangerous. The fact that, all too often, those who declined the "help" ended up on the business end of a torture rack only made things worse.

What people sought then, back in the day, was a concept of religious freedom that included the right to dissent. Unfortunately, the first proponents didn't close the circle. They sought freedom—but only for themselves. America's Puritan forbearers were known for their intolerance and their insistence that, even though the Church of England had gotten it wrong, they had gotten it right. The reason they threw Williams out was because he dared to tell them that maybe they too had got it wrong.

It took another generation to make the next great leap forward: Perhaps what's true for me isn't true for the guy down the street, across town, or even in the next town over. And maybe what he does behind the closed and private doors of his church doesn't affect me. Maybe his right to worship is as important as mine. Perhaps my right to worship as I see fit and his are strongly linked. Perhaps both will stand or fall together.

Maybe I'm not the best person to make moral decisions for another. Maybe I don't deserve that role. Maybe that's for the best.

That's the first step. Jefferson, Madison, and others took it a long time ago. Our problem today is that instead of trying to advance that step, too many people are working to reverse it.

2

RELIGION

In October of 2012, the Pew Forum on Religion and Public Life issued a survey on religious belief in America. Its core finding was startling: for the first time ever, the percentage of people who identified themselves as Protestants had dropped below 50 percent.[1]

The United States has never had an official religion, of course, but most scholars would agree that Protestantism in various forms had been the nation's dominant faith for a long time. So much so that references to it even infiltrated everyday speech. People speak of the "Protestant work ethic" that built this country and joke about the exalted role of WASPs—white, Anglo-Saxon Protestants—in running its affairs.

In popular histories, Protestantism tends to be portrayed somewhat monolithically, the better to contrast it with Catholicism, which didn't begin to gain a serious foothold in the United State until well into the nineteenth century.

That depiction fails to tell the whole story. Protestantism took various forms in America, and tension between rival denominations was apparent during the founding period. In fact, those tensions are what led, in part, to the separation of church and state. While some people at the time were thinking that separation would be good for relations between Catholics and Protestants or Christians and Jews, this was a lesser concern for the simple reason that there were not many Catholics and Jews around. The more-common thought was that dividing religion and government would bring peace to warring Protestant sects, which it did.

When I say "warring," I don't overstate the case. Protestant groups didn't get along back then. In chapter 1, I discussed James Madison's dismay at seeing Baptist preachers in Virginia sent to jail. They had been put there by the ruling Anglican establishment, which didn't brook dissent in matters of faith.[2]

Anglican establishments were common in many Southern states. In New England, Congregationalism—the remnants of the Puritan faith—dominated. Other colonies tended to favor a handful of Protestant denominations. In only one colony—Maryland—did Catholics have any real presence, and even there they were eventually outnumbered by Protestants.

These various Protestant factions didn't all get along. There were real differences in theology and how to approach God. Claims by today's religious Right that there was a "Christian" basis to American society would have made no sense to the founders or to many people of the colonial era. They could not agree on what was truly "Christian." A Quaker's god was not necessarily a Calvinist's god.

Key founders knew this. Thomas Jefferson discussed religion frequently with his friends. Jefferson never hesitated to take pot-shots at faith systems he found inscrutable. Although a believer, Jefferson had little use for rigid theologies such as Calvinism. His attempt to merge faith with a form of rationalism based on science and reason was seen as threatening to the reigning clergy of the day, who, much like today's religious Right activists, called for an embrace of biblical values.

The problem—then as now—is that no one can quite agree on what these biblical values are.

This is a long-running debate in America. The religious Right today tries to paper over this. Its use of terms like *Christian nation* or *Judeo-Christian heritage* is an attempt to imply that there was a time when a broad consensus concerning religion existed in American life. The assertion is that this consensus didn't break down until the modern era, when courts began enforcing a rigid separation of church and state, divorcing faith from public life.

This argument can't stand up to even casual scrutiny. American history is littered with examples of interfaith strife. One reads of Roger Williams fleeing Puritan Massachusetts and its intolerant theocracy, of Quakers hanged on Boston Common, of imprisoned Baptists, of Catholics denied the right to hold public office, and so on.

The startling thing about so many of these disputes is that they were among Christians. If there was a broad Christian consensus at that time, why were so many people fighting over religion?

Consider the donnybrook in Virginia, where James Madison led the charge against a proposal by Patrick Henry to use tax money to pay for "teachers of the Christian religion." Most Virginians were Christians, yet opposition to this scheme was swift and strong (and it sunk the proposal).

Why was opposition to Henry's idea so strong? One big reason is that Christians in Virginia knew they were divided. And they realized that a measure requiring all residents to pay for Christianity would, in effect, mean that some people would end up subsidizing versions of the Christian faith with which they strongly—perhaps violently—disagreed.

Madison realized this. In his famous broadside against Henry's bill, the "Memorial and Remonstrance against Religious Assessments," he observed that the measure "will destroy that moderation and harmony which the forbearance of our laws to intermeddle with Religion has produced among its several sects."[3]

Madison went on to add, "Torrents of blood have been spilt in the old world, by vain attempts of the secular arm, to extinguish Religious discord, by proscribing all difference in Religious opinion. Time has at length revealed the true remedy. Every relaxation of narrow and rigorous policy, wherever it has been tried, has been found to assuage the disease."[4]

Madison's reference to the Old World is to Europe, where for centuries Christians of various denominations had been slaughtering one another because they could not agree on matters of theology.

Consider also the Baptists of Danbury, Connecticut, whose letter to Jefferson sparked his famous reply endorsing a wall of separation between church and state. The Baptists were Christians, obviously. Yet they chafed at being forced to pay taxes to prop up the Congregational church in Connecticut—even though it was also a Christian denomination.

Christian, yes, but not the same type of Christian. That made all the difference. People felt very strongly about these differences, just as they do today. In speeches, I often remind people that the Church of Christ and the United Church of Christ both have the word *Christ* in their names and are both Christian denominations— and they agree on practically nothing.

This brings us to the flaw in the religious Right's "Christian nation" concept: it fails to answer the question, "What type of Christian?" Is it the Christianity of the Baptists or of the Anglicans? Is it the Christianity of the Puritans and their descendants or of the Catholics? Many years after the founding of America, it could have been the Christianity of the Mormons or of the Christian Scientists as well.

Many people active in the religious Right would not admit this, but the clear truth is that what they mean by a "Christian nation" is *my* version of Christianity.

As I was writing this book, a gentleman called me at the offices of Americans United for Separation of Church and State. He had seen the executive director of Americans United, Barry W. Lynn, on television and was distraught. He was convinced that Lynn was trying to drive religion from American life.

I was struck by something he said several times: "There must be some standard." By this he meant a religious standard, of course. Laws governing behavior and interactions between people, he argued, had to hew to a "standard."

My caller was a fundamentalist Christian. Thus, the standard he sought was one that just happened to dovetail with his own religious beliefs. How convenient!

This is a story as old as time. Over and over, the argument is made by religious fundamentalists and the ultraorthodox that their "standard" (i.e., their religion) should govern society and the behavior of others. Why? Because their religion is true.

As I've already mentioned, the obvious flaw in this thinking is that every orthodox believer is confident that he or she holds the one and only key to spiritual truth. This type of thinking is in no way unique to hard-line Catholic clerics or fundamentalist Protestants. One hears it in fundamentalists of every stripe—Christian, Muslim, Jewish, Hindu, and so on.

In fact, I am often amused (or perhaps I should say *alarmed*) by how much these groups sound alike when discussing social issues. You could strip away the theological references from an extreme Muslim cleric in Saudi Arabia who is talking about gay rights and easily conclude that you were listening to an American television evangelist. The ultraorthodox Jew who denies women's rights has a lot more in common with his fundamentalist Muslim and Christian counterparts than any of them would care to admit. They read from different scripts, but the result is the same.

Therein lies the problem with basing any society on a holy text: we're not really basing it on a holy text; we're basing it on *someone's interpretation* of a holy text. Those two concepts could not be any more different.

One of the things that is most tiresome about American political life is how often religious arguments are dragged into the political sphere as if they were some type of trump card. Far from being definitive, political arguments based on religion are the worst form of trump card because there's always someone else ready to throw down another card.

Over the centuries, Jesus has been portrayed as the best friend poor people ever had and their harshest critic. Some liberal Christians see Jesus as a kind of benign socialist who redistributes wealth. The religious Right sees him as a bootstrap capitalist who endorses dog-eat-dog economics.

Was Jesus for gun control? Believe it or not, I've heard people argue both sides of that question and each cited Bible passages.

During the Civil War, abolitionists in the North used the Bible to demand that all people be free. Southern ministers used the same book and found arguments advising slaves to obey their masters. In the modern era, segregationists and civil-rights advocates pointed to Bible passages to support their respective views.

It's not enough to say, "Well, one side is wrong." Both sides do say that; that's precisely my point. Both sides can point to Bible passages to promote their views. That's one reason our legal system isn't based on Bible passages.

Let's face it: Bible passages lead some people to unusual places. I mean no offense by saying that; it's just a rather obvious truth. A book as sprawling as the Bible, which was cobbled together over many hundreds of years and was compiled to serve many purposes, is by its very nature going to be open to lots of different interpretations. When I hear religious Right activists call for a "biblical" society, the first thing I think is, "According to whose interpretation?" (Hint: it will be theirs.)

Most religious conservatives, I've always believed, determine their opinion on a given matter first and then hunt for a Bible passage to back it up. People can be very creative here. Most people believe the Bible speaks to the need to care for the poor, and indeed Jesus himself didn't seem to own anything. Yet American theology has spawned an unusual aberration—the so-called prosperity Gospel. It's a uniquely American merger of Christianity with a get-rich-quick scheme, and it looks like rank heresy to many Christians—except for those who believe in it and point to Bible passages that they say buttress it. (Some argue that Jesus must have been rich; he had everything he needed and never worried about money.)

American politics is all too often a proof-texting contest because we stubbornly cling to this notion that a broad "Christian" or "Judeo-Christian" consensus can be reached. The thinking seems to be that such a consensus once existed, and that if we could just

find our way back to it, everything will be just fine. An entire political movement—the religious Right—is predicated on this belief.

Alas, there is no finding of something that never existed. We
can't get back to it; there's no "back" there. We have been arguing
about matters of theology for more than 220 years now. We don't
agree. That's kind of the point of America. We don't agree, so we
built a framework that allows us to disagree yet still live together in
peace. That framework is the First Amendment and its separation
of church and state.

But from day one, there have been those among us who didn't
agree with that framework. These are the people who believe that
since their religion is true, the state has the right, indeed the duty,
to embrace it. The rights of those who believe other things aren't
important because, well, those people are wrong. Error has no rights.

This attitude has persisted in America even as religious diversity has flourished. Framers like Jefferson and Madison would likely
look at the religious landscape of America today and smile warmly
at the range of options. Look at all of these choices. Our experiment
worked!

The theocratic legions from Jefferson's day would react much differently: so many ways to go wrong, so many ways to make a misstep,
so many roads to hell. Their spiritual descendants, adherents of
today's religious Right, look at America and say the same thing.

Those of us on the other side of the divide are frustrated by this
mind-set because it brings along an excessive amount of political
baggage and it seeks to control others. It's the very foundation of
those who seek to run the lives of strangers.

It's never enough for those belonging to the religious Right
to save their own skins; they've taken it upon themselves to
shield everyone else from the fires of hell. I understand the Great
Commission and their right to spread their view of the Gospels.
With their own money and resources, I say, let them have it. Again,
that is never enough for them.

The thing is, we've heard their message. Believe me, we've

heard it. They blare it at us from TV ministries, Christian radio, megachurch pulpits, publishing firms, websites, and so on. Message received. We got it.

Perhaps we're just not interested. Maybe some of us are just not worried about going to hell. Some Americans don't even believe there is such a place. Others figure it will be a welcome respite because there won't be any fundamentalists there. (My view has always been that a place full of uptight, sanctimonious fundamentalists can in no way be heaven for me. I'll pass.)

Religious fundamentalists sent the message; we heard it and consciously rejected it. In my view, they did all they were morally obligated to do. We'll take care of our souls from here.

Worse yet are the constant attempts by Christian fundamentalists to warp the law to meet their religious views. Having failed at persuading people to voluntarily adopt their religious views, they would enforce them by law.

To religious fundamentalists, I would say this: If you really believe same-sex marriage is a sin, then by all means don't marry someone of the same gender. If you encounter a same-sex couple and feel obligated to inform them that they are living a sinful lifestyle, go ahead. But if they persist (and I think they will), accept that you've done all you can and go home. Is your preaching really so weak—is your theological argument so bad—that you have to call on the resources of the state to enforce your theology?

Thankfully, Americans are increasingly rejecting this strict, fundamentalist mind-set. After a long period of right-wing, evangelical dominance, the pendulum appears to be moving in the other direction.

The evidence is found in a variety of polling data. Many Americans these days tell pollsters that they consider God too big of a concept for one religion. They see many paths to Heaven and tend to believe that what matters is not a by-rote expression of the proper religious practices but living a good life. This is anathema to many of today's theocrats.

At the same time, religious conservatives are panicking because current trends, if they continue, will eventually erode their grip on power. One of the reasons Protestants have dropped in number is that many people simply left organized religion. Pollsters call these people "nones" because, when asked to name their religion, they reply, "None."[5]

Nones should not be confused with atheists, agnostics, and humanists. The nonbelief community in the United States has always been very small, probably no more than 5 percent. Nones now account for 20 percent of the overall population, a stunning increase since the 1980s.

How do we account for this? As I said, most of the nones remain religious; they simply don't believe organized religion provides them with much.

Nones may blend religious traditions. They may take elements of Christianity and add Eastern thought. Some dabble in Earth-based spirituality. Such faiths may be highly individualized, but that does not make them any less meaningful for those who hold them.

Because no existing system truly reflects their beliefs or provides them with what they want, nones are honest in reporting that they have no formal spiritual home. I like to think they would gravitate to one of Jefferson's more famous quips, "I am of a sect by myself, as far as I know."

One can see the threat this poses to the leaders of conservative religious denominations. The audacity of homegrown spirituality could undermine the political power and financial well-being of these groups.

Yet the trend keeps growing, and it manifests itself in many ways. Consider the people who describe themselves as "spiritual but not religious." These individuals are often on the receiving end of attacks from both poles of the religious spectrum. Fundamentalists consider them peddlers of New Age flapdoodle while secularists fault them as closeted nonbelievers who are afraid to cut the final tie to religion.

Neither of these characterizations is accurate. I can't claim to be a spokesperson for this movement or its followers, but I don't have to be to realize that a yearning for spirituality has been a hallmark of American religious life from day one and that some of the nones are merely the latest manifestation of this. People today feel more secure in exploring boundless spirituality because they no longer have to fear the power of government intervention in the theological matters.

I've mentioned Roger Williams several times now. Williams was on a spiritual quest all his life. He started out as a Puritan minister, became a Baptist briefly, and ended up with no formal ties to any denomination. Was Williams "spiritual but not religious"? It depends on how you define the term *religious*. At a minimum, Williams was a man searching for answers and not finding them in any one system. You probably know someone like that today.

In the past, many people who could not find a comfortable fit with existing religious groups started their own movements. Joseph Smith founded the Church of Jesus Christ of Latter-Day Saints (Mormons). Mary Baker Eddy founded Christian Science. Ellen White founded the Seventh-Day Adventist Church.

Many of these movements were launched by a sudden and dramatic incident. Smith, for example, claimed that an angel appeared before him and directed him to a series of golden plates that contained sacred writings. Eddy had a revelation after being healed from a serious fall.

Most of those who seek "spirituality" today but not necessarily the rigid confines of religion don't want to start new movements. They simply want to take advantage of the religious liberty guaranteed in the First Amendment. This is an honest search for spiritual meaning that has a long track record in America. A person's right to do this should be celebrated, not ridiculed.

The problem is, the religious Right doesn't respect this process. On the most extreme wing of the religious Right sits a movement called Christian Reconstructionism, whose adherents argue that no one has a right to worship any god other than the Christian deity (again, as they define that being), and violations of this standard should be punishable by death.[6] (Naturally, the Reconstructionists can't agree on theology among themselves and have split into competing movements. Surprised?)

The Reconstructionists are a fringe movement. As we move down the line toward less extreme movements, we still find conservative religious leaders and groups that simply don't accept the idea of religious liberty as a concept that applies to all.

The irony is that there are real threats to religious freedom today—and the religious Right has been largely silent about them. An example is the rights of Muslims.

Jay Sekulow, an attorney hired by TV preacher Pat Robertson to run a religious Right legal group called the American Center for Law and Justice (ACLJ—clever, right?), constantly engages in Islamophobia and has an entire section of his group's website devoted to attacking the so-called Ground Zero mosque.[7]

There are a few problems with this name: The facility in question, while Islamic, is not merely a mosque—it's also a community center—and it's not at the Ground Zero site in New York City. It's three blocks away and would occupy space that formerly housed a department store.

Sekulow and others insisted that the mosque would somehow be an insult to the memory of those who died on September 11, 2001, even though the Sufi Muslims who sought to build it have nothing to do with the terrorist groups that sponsored the attack. In one especially incoherent column, Sekulow's son Jordan attacked mosque backers for daring to raise funds for the project during September of 2011—ten years after the attack.

The ACLJ claimed to be exploring legal options to stop construction of the Islamic center. It would be interesting to ask what those are since, generally speaking, religious groups in America have the right to buy property, conform to local zoning laws, and open facilities. (The project is currently on hold due to problems with fundraising.) Sekulow did this—all the while claiming to be an advocate of "religious freedom." It is a strange type of religious freedom that denies people their right to worship.

A similar incident occurred in Murfreesboro, Tennessee, where a group of local residents fought in court for years to stop a Muslim group from building a new mosque to replace a smaller, crowded structure.

In cases like this, people often try to mask their bigotry by raising issues relating to zoning or parking. The locals in Murfreesboro didn't even bother. They went into court and argued that they don't like Islam much. One of their more outlandish arguments was that Islam isn't really a religion.[8] It was creative but not clever, and it didn't go over too well in court. The mosque opened in August of 2012.

Sekulow's ACLJ is hardly the only religious Right group promoting Islamophobia. A right-wing, Catholic legal group called the Thomas More Law Center has a section on its website warning, "Radical Muslims and Islamic organizations in America take advantage of our legal system and are waging a 'Stealth Jihad' within our borders. Their aim is to transform America into an Islamic nation. They have already infiltrated the highest levels of our government, the media, our military, both major political parties, public schools, universities, financial institutions and the cultural elite."[9]

The sad thing about paranoid rhetoric like this is that it sounds very similar to the hysterical charges leveled against Catholics in the nineteenth century, when Protestant pastors warned darkly about plots by the pope to turn America into a Catholic nation under the control of the Vatican. (It also evokes the anti-Communist witch hunt of the 1950s. Does someone have a little list of all the Muslims who have infiltrated the top levels of government?)

In Oklahoma, right-wing groups whipped up so much hysteria over Islam that residents went to the polls in 2010 and approved a constitutional amendment to ban Islamic law in the state. The possibility of a Muslim takeover of Oklahoma always seemed somewhat remote, given that Muslims are a tiny minority there, and in the unlikely event it was ever tried, the First Amendment would protect the good people of the Sooner State from sharia. Voters passed the amendment anyway, 70 percent to 30 percent. It was quickly invalidated by a federal court.

What's especially alarming about all of this is that the very people who say and do these things designed to curb Islamic practices in America also claim to be defenders of religious freedom. It seems they don't have the faintest clue what religious freedom is. To them, religious freedom is their right to run the lives of others. But it apparently doesn't encompass the right of a religious group to buy land, meet local zoning laws, build a facility, and hold worship services there. This is a very odd definition of religious liberty.

Is it any wonder why so many Americans are wary of the vision of religious freedom espoused by the religious Right? All too often, the religious Right's version of religious freedom is the right to impose something on others. It is never satisfied with an individual's right to pray, read a religious book, or take part in some other type of religious activity. There always has to be some public expression, as if whole communities had a corporate right to sponsor a particular religion.

It's amazing how many people believe this. We see it manifested constantly in battles over things like religious displays on public property, the use of sectarian prayers before meetings of government bodies, the adoption of official proclamations calling on people to pray and read religious texts, and so on.

Government's first duty is to represent all of its citizens. It can't do that if it has a favorite religion or if it perceives its job is to make its citizens more religious.

As I've already discussed, many people these days are wary of conventional forms of religiosity. There are many reasons for this. Those reasons are less important than the effect this new development has on religious life in America.

I argue that a consensus on religion never existed—even among Christians. People feel too strongly about these matters. The closest we have ever come was through the adoption of so-called nonsectarian prayers or other measures that are seen as largely ceremonial and noncontroversial.

But even that "consensus," weak as it was, is breaking down. Nonbelievers rightly point out that even generic forms of religion exclude them. Many very devout people feel that a "one-size-fits-all" faith is bland and offensive. Some non-Christians argue that supposedly nonsectarian prayer still mimics the language and forms of Christianity.

Despite all of this, the promotion of such practices is highly valued by the members of the religious Right. They'll go to court to save them. But these things are not valid examples of religious freedom in action.

I've stressed many times that religious freedom is an individual right. It has a "corporate" expression only when bodies of believers join together in congregations for worship and fellowship. Those are voluntary associations. These bodies of believers are not the same as a town or a city. Municipalities have no religious-freedom rights. Attempts to shift the definition of religious freedom to include entire communities are dangerous. Altering our understanding of religious freedom as an individual right to a corporate/government one fosters a majority-rules vision of religious liberty that runs counter to what the Constitution mandates.

Think of it this way: the government has no power to compel anyone to recite "nonsectarian" prayers in private. How, then, can courts issue rulings telling state legislatures that they must limit their opening prayers to nonsectarian exercises (as the Supreme Court did in 1983)?

The answer is that what is being discussed here isn't religious freedom. It's something else, and even courts have admitted as much. Often, such prayers are referred to as a solemnizing exercise, or the claim is made that there is some nonreligious reason why prayer must be offered before the city council gets down to business.

We have come to a strange pass when prayers are described as nonreligious. And no one is fooled by this. Residents of these communities know exactly what is going on: prayers are being offered in the name of the community. Not everyone agrees with the content of those prayers or even if they ought to be uttered.

So if these fights aren't about religious freedom, what are they about? They are the last gasp of a religious majoritarianism that some have labored for years to elevate into law. Religious conservatives long ago lost direct support through taxation. They long ago lost the ability to determine who was fit to hold public office. They long ago lost the power to restrict the religious practices of groups they do not like.

But they haven't lost the power to remind people, as often as possible, that they once called the shots. Official prayers before the meetings of government bodies that are supposed to represent us all are an opportunity for one group to lord it over others—and they don't have the common decency to turn that down. Calling that "religious freedom" is an insult to the men and women who fought for that principle.

It would be remiss of me to leave this topic without touching on two canards about religious belief in America commonly circulated by the religious Right.

The first is that religious freedom was crafted only for Christian groups, or that it doesn't cover nonbelievers.

This is simply wishful thinking on the part of the right wing. Nothing in the historical record supports this view, and much debunks it. No language in the Constitution states or even implies that its protections are for Christians only. It's clear from the writings of the founders that they perceived religious freedom as wide ranging. If you doubt this, read George Washington's letter to the Touro Synagogue—and recall that it was written prior to the adoption of the Bill of Rights.

To reject Washington's vision is to believe that there is a hierarchy of religions in America, that some are genuine and some are not. While some in the religious Right undoubtedly believe this (and are certain their faith rests at the top), nothing in the law buttresses this view. A religion does not have more legal rights behind it simply because it has more adherents.

It is sometimes difficult to get this point across in the culture. But that is why we have a First Amendment. Occasionally, our courts are charged with the task of bringing the culture and the law into alignment.

A good example is found in Wicca and Paganism, two nature-based faiths that some scholars say are growing in America. I have been amazed at how many people believe that these religions have lesser rights simply because they aren't as well known as, say, Presbyterianism or Lutheranism.

Sometimes, this misunderstanding comes from high places. In 2006, Americans United for Separation of Church and State sued the Department of Veterans Affairs after officials there refused to allow a Wiccan woman whose husband had been killed in combat in Afghanistan to put a Wiccan symbol on his grave marker. The man in question was Wiccan, so adding the symbol would have seemed to be the right thing to do. Yet officials at the VA denied the request, insisting that the Wiccan pentagram was not on their list of "approved" symbols. (The VA reversed its policy as soon as litigation was filed.)[10]

In 2012, Americans United assisted a Wiccan priestess in Virginia who sought to register with local officials so she could preside at weddings, a routine matter for other members of the clergy. She was denied and told by officials that she had to have a building to worship in. (Wiccans often meet outdoors or in private homes.) Clearly this was not the standard, as many clergy who perform weddings in Virginia are retired or no longer lead a congregation. The matter was cleared up after attorneys from Americans United wrote to local officials.[11]

A second claim is that American law and the Constitution protect only freedom of religion, not freedom from religion.

In my business, one hears this assertion a lot. It has become a type of slogan for many on the Far Right, and even some politicians have adopted it. They probably think it's clever. It's not; it's insipid.

First off, of course the First Amendment protects the right to be an atheist as much as it protects the right to be a believer. No court ruling has ever cast doubt on this idea.

More to the point, as I've noted in writings elsewhere, this slogan rests on a false premise. The implication is that only a nonbeliever would wish to be free from religion. But this is not so. Under the right conditions, we all want to be from religion—at least, certain expressions of religion. If you're not a Jehovah's Witness, there's a reason for that: you choose not to be.

Would you sit by idly if your local public school started teaching Scientology to your child in class? Probably not. It sounds like you want to be free from that, and if you were not raised in that faith and don't consider it your own, that's perfectly understandable.

What if your town council was dominated by Zoroastrians who opened every meeting with a fire ritual to honor Ahura Mazda? You might want to be free from that—or at least free from the assumption that the council's actions represented your theological views.

It's especially ironic to hear religious Right activists spout this line, given the large number of religions they seek to be free from. Many Americans these days have adopted an open spirituality that allows them to see the value in the rituals and practices of other faiths. As I was writing this book, for example, a story circulated on news websites about non-Catholics (and even some atheists) who decided to give up something for Lent because the idea of making a sacrifice and perhaps living a simpler life appealed to them.

This sort of thing is heresy to those on the religious Right, who continue to insist that only their narrow version of faith is pleasing to God and that you can't just dip your toe into faith, you need full immersion. (But again, they can't agree on what that worship is. Put two fundamentalists in a room, and I guarantee you, they'll start squabbling over doctrine within five minutes.) Other religions are seen as having nothing to offer.

I don't dispute anyone's right to believe this. What I dispute is the attempt to lord it over the rest of us by establishing it as the standard under which everyone must live.

3

SEX

Religious conservatives' long-running obsession with the sex lives of others is, to be frank, more than a little creepy.

For much of human history, ultraconservative religious leaders and their followers have attempted to control what consenting adults do sexually, how they do it, and with whom they do it. For a long time, this clampdown on sexuality had an added benefit: it allowed religious leaders to control reproduction and child rearing.

The invention of safe, affordable, and effective forms of birth control in the modern era upset the power of the ultraconservatives and ignited a culture war that continues to this day. It did this by decoupling sex from pregnancy; inevitably, this led to a freer and more open attitude about sex. Of course, people had been engaging in premarital sex prior to the invention of the birth-control pill and other contraceptives, but in those cases where pregnancy was the result, marriage often followed. Reduction of worries about pregnancy in turn reduced the need for so-called shotgun weddings.

Premarital sex is now nearly universal in the United States. According to a 2006 study by the Guttmacher Institute, 95 percent of people in the United States engage in sex prior to marriage. Interestingly, Guttmacher also found that this was not a new trend, noting that among women born in the 1940s, 90 percent engaged in sex before marriage.[1]

To the religious Right, figures like this are nothing short of scandalous. That consenting adults might want to partake in these experiences is, for many reasons, threatening to religious conservatives.

A good deal of conspiratorial thinking exists in the world of the religious Right. Most people, looking at the changes that have occurred within American society since the 1960s—including greater sexual freedom and the liberation of women—would attribute those changes to the evolution of cultural norms.

Indeed, a study of history shows that these changes weren't just foisted on the country by the Supreme Court; they had antecedents. Women began agitating for more rights in the late nineteenth century, and the suffragettes won the right to vote at the federal level in 1920 after a lengthy campaign. At the same time, some people were arguing for greater sexual liberty, although this movement was less high profile. As decades went by, these ideas won greater acceptance. Thus, court rulings in this area in the 1960s weren't so much an aberration, then, as a reflection of shifting cultural norms.

Instead of accepting this history, the religious Right instead sees conspiracy. Thus, societal shifts such as these are often attributed to liberal courts that supposedly sought to remake American society. A few key Supreme Court cases, in particular, are singled out for special disdain and scorn.

Many young Americans take the availability of birth control as a given. They forget (or do not know) how successful conservative religious lobbies have been in restricting access to birth control over the years. This is unfortunate because it can lead to a type of complacency.

To understand where we are now, we must know where we have been. The ability to access safe, reliable forms of birth control didn't just appear one day. It was a hard-fought right. There are some today who still believe it was a mistake; they'd love nothing better than to drag our country back to a less-free time, a time when powerful, conservative, religious interests had an inordinate amount of control over all of us.

Prior to the invention of the birth-control pill, devices intended to prevent pregnancy were limited and their effectiveness was spotty—but they did exist. Condoms, for example, have been used as far back as ancient times, often made of animal bladders. The invention of the vulcanization of rubber by Charles Goodyear in 1844 led to the creation of rubber condoms, which, although thick and somewhat brittle, were effective if properly used. Latex condoms, which were increasingly common by 1920, were another step forward.

Women had access to various devices to block access to the cervix, and foams and spermicides were also available. Even in ancient times, women knew that some plants could be used as contraceptives, among them, Queen Anne's lace and silphium, a plant that is now extinct probably due to overuse. (In addition, nineteenth-century quacks often marketed preparations that they claimed served as contraceptives. They didn't work, but their existence indicates that the demand was there.)

The hierarchy of the Catholic Church lobbied to restrict access to all contraceptive devices and medications. Many Protestant leaders did as well. Most Protestant denominations would later drop their opposition to birth control. The Catholic hierarchy never did.

It's important to understand that church officials sought to ban birth control even for married couples and non-Catholics and that this continued until the 1960s. In addition, the laws that church officials pushed to pass didn't just outlaw birth control, they also forbade information *about* birth control. Well into the twentieth century, in some states, a married couple could ask a doctor for advice about how best to limit the size of their family and be told that he could not legally distribute such information. Laws like this were common throughout the nineteenth and into the twentieth century in New England states, which had a strong Catholic tradition.

Naturally, many people chafed at these restrictive provisions. In Connecticut, the laws were enforced only sporadically, but the existence of them on the books rankled many advocates of birth control; these advocates decided to test the law.

In 1961, a birth-control advocate named Estelle Griswold joined forces with Charles Lee Buxton, a doctor and the chair of the Department of Obstetrics at Yale Medical School, to open a clinic in New Haven that, among other things, offered advice and counseling about contraceptives. No actual birth-control devices were distributed at the clinic, but the state's Catholic leaders still perceived it as a threat and demanded it be shut down. State officials promptly raided the facility and arrested Griswold and Buxton.

Of course, that was just what the two wanted. Griswold and Buxton challenged the state's action in court. Their case went all the way to the US Supreme Court. In 1965, the high court handed down a landmark ruling, striking down Connecticut's anti-birth-control law in the case *Griswold v. Connecticut.*[2]

"Would we allow the police to search the sacred precincts of marital bedrooms for telltale signs of the use of contraceptives?" asked Justice William O. Douglas for the seven-member high-court majority. "The very idea is repulsive to the notions of privacy surrounding the marriage relationship. We deal with a right of privacy older than the Bill of Rights."[3]

Although it's not as well known as some of the Supreme Court's other notable decisions, *Griswold* is an extremely important ruling. In the decision, the high court made note of the existence of a zone of privacy that governs human sexual behavior. It is not within the power of government, the court ruled, to invade this zone and meddle in our most intimate and private affairs.

This principle seems utterly noncontroversial to most Americans today—but that's only because so many people grew up or came of age in the post-*Griswold* world. To most people, the right to determine the size of your family (or if you want to have one at all) and the ability to control your own sex life is a given. These ideas are, in part, the fruits of *Griswold,* and they make perfect sense to most Americans today. To the religious Right, they are an abomination.

Part of this is due to the long-running aversion religious fundamentalists have to any sexual activity that does not result in procreation. But there's more to the story.

Fundamentalist religions tend to be patriarchal. They look on any innovation or societal change that results in greater autonomy

and decision making for women with great suspicion. It is difficult to think of an invention that resulted in greater autonomy for
women than the birth-control pill.

So ubiquitous it is now known simply as "the pill," oral contraceptive medication has been called one of the most significant
inventions of the twentieth century. It's hard to argue with that.
Prior to the invention of the pill—an affordable, safe, and effective
form of birth control—women were often at the mercy of regular
cycles of childbearing and child rearing.

Anyone who reads even casually in history knows how this
played out. Fertile women often endured sequential pregnancies,
with their lives defined by this experience. (In an age before effective medicine, most families endured the death of at least one child,
sometimes several.) Such a system made women economically
dependent on men.

By giving women and their partners the power to space births
apart and to plan children, the pill offered a form of emancipation.
Large families were still an option for those who wanted them, but
for those who did not, a new world of options was suddenly open.

The pill put decision making in the hands of women in another
important way: it was an effective contraceptive aimed squarely at
them. No longer did a woman have to rely on a man and hope he
would make the decision to use some form of birth control, such as
agree to wear a condom. She had the power in the palm of her hand
(often literally).

It is difficult to underestimate the scope of this development
and the threat it posed to religious conservatives. For centuries,
conservative religious interests had used reproduction to control
women and accord them second-class status in society. Suddenly
that power was stripped away. A backlash was inevitable.

Worse yet, from the perspective of the religious Right, the
Supreme Court began expanding the rights outlined in *Griswold*. In
1972, the court extended the *Griswold* ruling to unmarried couples,
encompassing them in the zone of privacy outlined in that decision.

In another crushing blow to the right wing, the high court held that what consenting adults do concerning reproduction was simply no business of the state or large religious lobbies.[4]

Griswold's zone of privacy would return to haunt the religious Right again. It was cited in 1973's *Roe v. Wade*, which struck down state antiabortion laws, and in *Lawrence v. Texas*, a 2003 decision that invalidated laws banning homosexual acts between consenting adults.

With a track record like this, it's easy to see why the religious Right despises *Griswold.* In its view, the *Griswold* decision ushered in numerous evils: it chiefly liberated women, it gave sexual license, and it allowed for gay liberation.

But *Griswold*, from the perspective of members of the religious Right, stands for much more. It is, in many ways, a rebuke of their vision of America. The religious Right's America is an America where women know their place, gays remain invisible, and sex outside of marriage doesn't happen.

Griswold upset this tidy applecart. Of course, *Griswold* didn't result in or force a change in societal attitudes. It would be easy to argue that *Griswold* reflected changing attitudes and didn't drive them. The point is, the attitudes began to change, and *Griswold*, by codifying these changes in the law, greatly pushed things along. The America that the religious Right had assumed would endure forever—the America that, for so long, granted religious conservatives the right to tell others what to do—wasn't just challenged, it was turned on its head.

To younger Americans, all of this seems like so much ancient history. They have a difficult time imagining an America where birth control is illegal. Surely such things are in the realm of fantasy, straight out of *The Handmaid's Tale*, right?

Perhaps. But as recent events have proven, religious conservatives have yet to make their peace with birth control. A new attack would come, and when it did, it would assume a most unexpected form: it would come cloaked in the noble garment of religious freedom.

President Barack Obama's healthcare-reform law was a complex piece of legislation, to be sure. But one of its aims was fairly simple: to ensure that all Americans had access to at least a baseline healthcare plan.

The law, as interpreted by officials in the US Department of Health and Human Services (HHS), mandated that all firms providing health insurance include birth control among the coverage.

To insurance companies, this made sense. It's cheaper to provide birth control than to pay for unplanned births. The state of Texas learned this the hard way in 2012 when, at the behest of the Far Right, legislators voted to cut off funding to Planned Parenthood. The state bragged that it had saved $73 million in family-planning services. This was before lawmakers learned that the state would have to spend at least $270 million due to an uptick in unplanned births among poor women.

Since the use of birth control has become common, providing it in employee plans made sense from the employees' standpoint as well. Statistics show that at some point in their lives, the vast majority of women (a percentage in the high nineties) will use birth control for at least some period of time. This is not surprising when you consider two factors: (1) most straight women get married, and (2) a woman's fertility can start in her teen years and last into her forties.

The regulations promulgated by the HHS exempted houses of worship and ministries. Religiously affiliated institutions that serve the public (such as hospitals, universities, and charities) were accommodated by shifting the cost for birth control from the employer to the insurance companies. (Again, the thinking was that insurers would be happy to pay for contraceptives over births, and they were.)

The Catholic bishops immediately asserted that this was not enough. They were soon joined by the (largely Protestant) religious Right in insisting that their religious-freedom rights were under attack. In addition, a slew of lawsuits was filed by private employers who insisted that they should not be compelled to provide an insurance plan that includes birth control. These cases were bankrolled by religious Right legal groups with deep pockets.

Take a minute to consider the argument being made here. These employers—who were involved in secular operations such as mining, retail sales, manufacturing, and other enterprises that have nothing to do with transmitting faith—asserted that someone else's decision to use birth control violated their religious liberty.

Remember, the healthcare law doesn't require anyone to use birth control. It merely makes it available (through private insurers) for those who want it. In this case, any cost born by these secular firms is incidental. It's folded into a much larger fee assessed for providing health insurance.

More to the point, private actions undertaken by an employee of a secular firm simply can't infringe on that employer's religious freedom—that is, unless that private action consists of standing in the door of a church, trying to prevent the employer from entering.

If the bishops' version of religious freedom carries the day, millions of Americans who work for companies that have nothing to do with religion could lose access to contraceptives simply because their bosses object to it. This would be a rather remarkable turn of events: your medical rights could hinge on where your boss goes to church.

Worse yet, poor families would take the hardest hit. The cost of birth control varies depending on the type of method used. Birth-control pills can cost as little as $9 a month for generics, but not all women can use those pills. Some need brand-specific medication, which can easily run $100 or more per month. The most convenient and effective forms of birth control—intrauterine devices (IUDs) and implants that can prevent pregnancy for up to ten years—are also the most expensive because they require surgical intervention. Some insurance plans won't pay for that.

Some birth-control opponents have objected to providing it through insurance plans and have argued that it's no big deal if they don't because birth control is cheap. Such thoughtless statements are further examples of the growing disconnect between corporate officials (who, at larger companies, often receive salaries in six or seven figures) and their workers (many of whom just scrape by). For the bosses, $100 a month is pocket change; for their workers, it's anything but.

The money issue is important, but the crux of the matter remains this: a worker's decision to use birth control in no way prevents the boss or owner of the firm from going to the house of worship of his choice. It in no way stops him from praying, reading the religious text of his choice, or joining with like-minded believers for fellowship.

As I mentioned in chapter 1, imagine a standard like this in action for other religions. Members of the Church of Scientology dispute the value of psychiatric counseling.[5] Should a Scientologist who owns a retail establishment be permitted to deny his employees all forms of psychological counseling and drugs, such as antidepressants?

Should a boss who happens to be a Jehovah's Witness be permitted to exclude all forms of surgery from a health plan because surgery often involves blood transfusions? More to the point, why not allow a biblical-literalist boss to deny his employees a health-care plan entirely? After all, they're supposed to rely on prayer alone for healing.

The right that religious conservatives are seeking here has little to do with religious liberty. It is, in fact, a right to control others and tell them what to do—to be the boss of them both on the job and off.

It's important in cases like this to look at what lies beneath. The Catholic hierarchy hasn't even been able to persuade its own members to listen to them on the matter of birth control. Millions of American Catholics sit in the pews, listen to clergy fulminate against contraceptives, and go right on using them.

So why are the bishops and their friends in the religious Right going to the mat over a fight they have clearly lost?

The simple answer is that change is hard, and it's especially hard for members of top-heavy, patriarchal religions. As I've noted, safe, affordable, and effective birth control ushered in a new era in America. It really did change the culture. Many religious leaders have yet to come to grips with that.

For women, the ability to control their reproduction is the ability to control their destinies. When women gained this power, the old order began to change. Conservative clerics, who had been calling the shots on this matter for something like fifteen hundred years, saw their grip slip. Is it any wonder they would fight this? Is it any wonder they would grasp at any reed that might give them back a semblance of the power over women they once enjoyed? The birth-control controversy of 2012 gave them that shot.

What's exasperating about this to many people is that the new attack on birth control simply ignores the reality of how most Americans live their lives. As I've pointed out, use of birth control is ubiquitous. It simply makes no sense to erect barriers to its access and use, especially for young people.

Some argue that this isn't relevant to the debate. All that matters, they say, is that those who object to birth control have a sincere belief that its use is wrong. If they genuinely hold that belief, the argument goes, then their rights must be respected.

This argument has at least two gaping flaws: (1) it has never been the standard in America, and (2) it would be impossible to implement.

In a free society, people believe all manner of things with great sincerity. Sincerity isn't the issue; the issue is how those sincere beliefs, or, more accurately, the actions that flow from them, affect the larger society.

The Supreme Court has ruled repeatedly that actions posing a threat to others—even if those actions are based in religion—can be curtailed. This is one of the reasons why, for example, snake handling is illegal: it exposes people to injury and death.

Jehovah's Witnesses used to compel children to work long

hours, peddling religious literature on the streets. Courts ruled that states could use anti-child-labor laws to stop this activity (or at least reduce the hours). The right of children to be free from long work hours outweighs the religious-freedom rights of the Witnesses.[6]

Some fundamentalists refuse to take their children to doctors, asserting that they have a religious-freedom right to rely on faith healing alone. Courts have not been sympathetic to this argument. Especially in the case of serious illness, courts have ordered that medical treatment be supplied. The child's right to life overrules the religious-freedom rights of the parents.

Some might argue that access to birth control does not rise to this level. Why wouldn't it? Birth control isn't just a "lifestyle" issue. It is medication. In some cases, it is used for reasons other than the prevention of births. Some women need birth-control pills to shrink ovarian cysts or to treat endometriosis or menstrual cramps. It's hard to imagine any other drug being subjected to someone else's religious-liberty veto. Even Viagra, which really is more of a "lifestyle" drug, isn't subjected to this type of control by religious groups.

Even if birth control is being used solely to limit births, why isn't this a compelling reason to override another party's religious objection? The Supreme Court ruled some years ago that the government has the power to overrule religious-liberty claims in the face of a compelling state interest.[7] In recent years, this standard has actually been made tighter, with the high court asserting that laws that are neutral on their face and generally applicable can be applied to religious groups as well.

Congress did pass a law in 1994 designed to restore the "compelling state interest" standard. But this legislation—the Religious Freedom Restoration Act—was seen as an effort to protect the right of individuals to practice their own faith, not to impose it on others or to control their behavior.

In other cases, accommodations can be worked out that respect the rights of all involved. A case in point comes from Kentucky, where a court ruled that the state had the right to require an old-order Amish group to display bright-orange safety triangles on their horse-drawn vehicles.

Government officials argued that dark, slow-moving vehicles presented a hazard, especially at dawn or dusk on narrow back roads. The triangles were a good-faith effort to prevent accidents. Some Amish groups protested, arguing that the orange triangle was "loud" and "worldly." The triangle, they said, offended their plain lifestyle.

After some Amish men spent time in jail for refusing to display the triangle, legislators began discussing a compromise. The Amish who protested were offended by the triangle, but they weren't bothered by reflective tape, lanterns, and red reflectors. They agreed to use these items on their buggies, easing safety concerns. (Nevertheless, conservative lawmakers in Kentucky used the controversy to push a restrictive "religious liberty" law through the legislature designed to give people a legal right to discriminate against others or impose their faith on them.)[8]

Can a compromise be reached in the birth-control debate? President Obama has certainly tried. One thing he proposed was shifting payment for birth control from religious nonprofits to the insurance companies. (Remember, houses of worship are exempt entirely from the requirement to provide access to birth control.) The bishops rejected this compromise. They asserted that they would accept nothing less than an exemption for all religiously affiliated institutions (including hospitals, colleges, etc.) and, furthermore, demanded that *every private individual* with a religious belief against contraception be granted the same right, even if the business he or she owns is wholly secular.

The bishops weren't truly interested in compromise. In fact, they never gave so much as an inch on their demands. The president and the HHS officials moved toward the bishops more than once. But the bishops never moved from their position. This is not compromise.

Why wouldn't the bishops bend even a tiny bit? Because their goal was to restrict access to birth control for as many people as possible due to the fact that their hierarchy (and it is the hierarchy, not the church membership) opposes the use of birth control.

In a sense, the bishops must have looked at Obama's healthcare law with a certain amount of amazement. Suddenly an issue that had remained dormant for many years—access to birth control—was very much alive again. And to boot, the bishops were presented with a legal avenue to achieve one of their long-standing goals: twisting US policy on contraceptives to meet their narrow theological beliefs, beliefs that are out of step with something like 95 percent of the church's own members. That they were able to do this while seizing the moral high ground and claiming to be standing up for religious freedom is nothing short of remarkable.

The bishops' anti-birth-control salvo is all the more astounding when one considers the state of their social service, medical, and education networks. These are heavily funded by the taxpayer. In some parts of the country, Catholic Charities receives 70 percent of its budget from taxpayers. It provides services to people of all faiths and of none, but it insists on subjecting its employees, many of whom are not even Catholic, to church strictures on birth control.

The same situation exists at Catholic colleges and hospitals. These entities are massively funded by the taxpayer and hire many non-Catholics. It's a most curious dichotomy: When the bishops are seeking to raid the public purse, they portray their institutions are quasi-public, willing to serve all and open to hiring from many religious traditions. Yet these same institutions become church property and inviolable when it comes to meeting even a miniscule government regulation, such as allowing people to make their own decisions about reproduction and sexuality.

The Catholic hierarchy has a rather creative view of religious freedom. To them, it's the right to rake in taxpayer support with virtually no oversight. In 2012, the Obama administration decided not to renew a federal grant that had been extended to the church to combat human trafficking. The church had parceled out the money to a series of subcontractors, and there was a problem: the subcontractors were told not to offer any contraceptives or reproductive healthcare to victims of trafficking.

To many people, this simply didn't make sense and was, in fact, poor public policy. Victims of trafficking may have been raped or forced into prostitution. Some of them desperately needed the very services the church chose to deny them. Yet when the grant was not renewed, church officials screamed that their religious freedom was being violated and that they were the victims of an anti-Catholic plot. In the minds of some bishops, it seems, the government's failure to fund a church project is a violation of the church's religious liberty. (One often hears this argument when it comes to taxpayer funding of Catholic secondary schools. See more in the chapter on education.)

Religious conservatives' refusal to face the realities of modern sexuality is more than just prudish; it has real-world effects—all of them negative. Under their warped view of religious freedom, for example, many public schools are reluctant to offer meaningful sex-education classes.

The situation is similar to the teaching of creationism in public schools: the right being elevated isn't religious freedom, it's the right to be ignorant. Thanks to pressure from the religious Right, what passes for sex education in many public schools probably does more harm than good. It many communities, it's not fair to call what is offered "sex education" because it isn't really about sex and it doesn't educate.

Rather than face reality—that most people have sex before marriage and that many teens are sexually active—religious conservatives for years have pounded the drum for abstinence over and over. They've done this even though the percentage of people who remain abstinent prior to marriage is miniscule and despite the fact that polls show a majority support more comprehensive forms of sex education in public schools.

This is a case where, thanks to misguided views from the religious Right, the will of the people is simply ignored. For many years, federal money funded solely "abstinence only" programs. As the name implies, such programs stress the idea of refraining from sex until marriage, so no information about contraceptives is offered. Actually, that's not quite accurate. Information is offered about contraceptives, and it's usually inaccurate and designed to discourage the use of such devices.

The main problem with abstinence-only education is that it's unrealistic. As I've mentioned, the vast majority of people in America have sex prior to marriage—remember, the figure is 95 percent, according to the Guttmacher Institute. Many of the abstinence-only programs attempt to deal with this by employing a fear-based model: if you have sex, you'll die, get sick, or experience some other horrible outcome. Of course, most teens know people (including their parents) who have had sex prior to marriage and are not dead because of it, so the approach leaves a little to be desired.

Throughout the 1980s and '90s and during the George W. Bush presidency, federal law funded abstinence-only programs in many states under a law known as the Adolescent Family Life Act and other programs. By the end of Bush's presidency, this funding had reached $204 million per year, syndicated columnist Ellen Goodman reported early in 2009.[9]

The problem is, abstinence programs simply do not work. Goodman and other writers pointed to a study by a Johns Hopkins researcher who looked at two groups of teenagers—one group of teens who took a pledge of abstinence, and one group of teens who did not. The teens were of similar backgrounds for control purposes. This researcher found no difference in their sexual behavior, except for one damning area: members of the group who had taken the abstinence vow were much less likely to use birth control, especially condoms, during sex. The findings here buttressed previous studies that found much the same thing: abstinence-only education did little to ensure abstinence.[10]

These findings should have shocked religious conservatives. After all, they carp incessantly about teen pregnancy and the abortion rate among teen girls. One thing that might lower that rate is effective and regular use of contraceptives, which many conservatives undercut by their support of abstinence programs.

Under President Obama, federal funding began shifting to programs that favor a more comprehensive approach, where abstinence is stressed but condoms and others forms of birth control are discussed. Polls show this is the type of sex education most Americans support. But federal money still funds some abstinence programs. The money, although reduced, has been inserted into healthcare legislation by congressional conservatives every year. They usually tack it onto a larger piece of legislation where it can't be easily removed.

Federal funding tells only part of the story. Many public schools, especially in conservative areas, choose to forgo federal money and implement their own sex-education programs. Many of these programs are just more fear-based moralizing, sometimes augmented by a dose of fundamentalist preaching. It doesn't work there either. Some of the highest teen-pregnancy rates are in the Bible Belt. According to the Guttmacher Institute, of the ten states with the highest teen-pregnancy rates, six are in fundamentalist strongholds: Mississippi, Texas, Arkansas, Louisiana, Oklahoma, and Georgia. Three New England states often derided as hopelessly liberal by the Far Right—Vermont, Maine, and Massachusetts— have teen-pregnancy rates that scrape the bottom.

The final area where sexuality and claims of religious freedom clash is gay rights. According to the bishops and their allies in the religious Right, religious freedom means they have the right to discriminate against some people—mainly members of the LGBTQ community. Religious groups do have the right to engage in some forms of discrimination, but the right is not as widespread as they may think. In addition, rights asserted by a church do not necessarily carry over to a private individual operating in a purely secular environment.

While many churches are accepting of gays and lesbians, the hierarchy of the Catholic Church and its fundamentalist allies remain rooted in the homophobic camp. Naturally, they seek to elevate their increasingly fossilized policies into the law of the land for all to follow.

The bishops are careful not to engage in the crude gay bashing that has been the hallmark of the religious Right. They go out of their way to stress the need to respect the individual and maintain that it is not being gay that's the problem, it's acting on it. But at the end of the day, this is cold comfort to most LGBTQ Americans. The bishops may employ lofty language, but the result of their policies for gays and lesbians remains the same: second-class status and discrimination.

The growing acceptance of LGBTQ rights in America, including same-sex marriage, has put religious fundamentalists in a difficult spot. Their views are increasingly out of step with the average American. As they see their position becoming increasingly anachronistic, they are desperately casting about for some way to preserve their right to discriminate and treat people as second-class citizens on the basis of their sexuality. Again, a bogus religious-freedom argument is being raised.

Some of the arguments employed reek of desperation. Religious groups occasionally assert that the spread of LGBTQ rights, especially same-sex marriage, will compel their churches to offer services to gay people.

This argument is so bad that I'm surprised some even raise it. The short answer is that this will never happen, not as long as we have a First Amendment. Under that provision, houses of worship have an absolute right to determine who can join and who can partake in services.

A Catholic church is under no obligation to offer its religious services to all comers. The church can—and does—impose various conditions on the receipt of its services. For example, an opposite-sex, non-Catholic couple could not demand the right to be married

in a Catholic church. Nor could an interfaith couple. Church officials may require such couples to undergo religious instruction or
conversion before agreeing to preside at their weddings.

Same-sex couples would face an absolute bar when approaching
churches that don't sanction such unions. To be sure, such couples
would be free to work for change within the church or rally
members and clergy to ask for change, but legally they would have
no recourse.

What really seems to be bothering some religious groups is that
the cultural winds are shifting, and they are worried about being
labeled as bigoted and backward. The Catholic bishops admitted as
much in a legal brief they filed before the Supreme Court in 2013.[11]
The court was considering two cases dealing with same-sex marriage, and the bishops' legal arm weighed in with a brief that made
a most remarkable argument.

Basically, the bishops asserted that if same-sex marriage were
to win state sanction in America, religious groups that oppose it
would be on the outs and would be looked upon with disfavor. They
might even lose access to government benefits.

By *benefits*, the bishops probably meant the lucrative, taxpayer-
funded contracts their church has come to rely on. Essentially, the
bishops are arguing that if they are perceived to be bigots, their
access to the taxpayer spigot would be jeopardized.

What they fail to grasp is that if there is indeed a cultural shift
under way, the Supreme Court or any arm of government can't save
the church hierarchy. Sixty years ago, it wasn't uncommon to hear
some pastors, especially in the South, parrot white-supremacist
views and attack interracial marriage. Today, only the rankest bigot
does such things. Whether the bishops care to acknowledge it or
not, the day is probably coming when pulpit attacks on same-sex
marriage will grate on American ears as much as criticisms of
interracial marriage do today. This is going to happen regardless
of what the courts, Congress, or the president says.

As always, it's useful in cases like this to take a step back and ponder what lies beneath the surface. Over the years, I've had occasion to attend gatherings hosted by groups within the religious Right, and I've read the publications and web postings produced by these groups. The constant gay bashing makes the mind reel. The more-extreme groups often imply that the very fate of Western civilization is at stake and that the extension of rights to LGBTQ Americans will result in the destruction of the nation.

You hear religious Right leaders spout arguments that aren't even remotely persuasive. Members of the religious Right, for example, cherry-pick the Bible. They point to a passage in the Book of Leviticus that they say bans homosexual behavior but then conveniently overlook a host of other rules in that same book that very few people abide by today (such as complex dietary regulations and bans on wearing clothing of mixed fibers).

More to the point, they ignore the Bible's prohibition on divorce. Actually, the right-wing evangelical response to divorce is telling. Those on the religious Right love to come up with what they think are clever slogans—"God made Adam and Eve, not Adam and Steve,"—as they proclaim their belief that marriage is one man and one woman for life.

Many of them have the one-man-and-one-woman part down. The "for life" business has been giving them some trouble. Bible Belt divorce rates are notoriously high, and statistics show that evangelicals divorce at the same rate as everyone else, even at a tad higher rate, according to some surveys.

The Bible could celebrate divorce, and it still would not matter. The biblical argument is irrelevant. United States law is not based on what the Bible says (or, more accurately, on what some people *believe* the Bible says). We're a secular republic, not a theocracy.

Other arguments, especially those against same-sex marriage, are an attempt at misdirection. Whenever the same-sex-marriage issue comes up, religious conservatives are quick to make claims that marriage can't be "redefined" by the state because it is about raising children, and every child deserves a mother and a father.

Where to begin? For starters, the state can and does redefine marriage. What else would you call the ban on polygamy that now exists in virtually every Western nation? Polygamy has long roots in history. It goes back to at least the time of the Old Testament. For various reasons, it fell out of favor in the West and is no longer permitted. Some would argue that this was the original attempt to redefine marriage.

Issues of child rearing are merely an attempt by the Far Right to muddy the waters, an effort to shift the argument from the question of whether it's just to deny marriage to same-sex couples to a plaintive cry of "Someone please think of the children."

No objective studies show that same-sex parenting is harmful for children. But there is one thing that virtually every study does show is bad for children: poverty. Many of us wish conservatives spent even half the time opposing it that they do battling marriage equality.

Furthermore, procreation is not a necessary predicate to marriage. If it were, infertile couples, elderly couples, and couples who don't wish to have children could be denied the right to marry.

The child-rearing argument is a distraction. LGBTQ Americans are seeking the right to marry, not the right to raise children. They already have the latter. The focus is on marriage because this is the right being denied. And it's not just a right—it's the whole host of benefits that come with that right.

Consider just one of these rights: hospital visitations. Imagine a couple that has been together for forty years. Imagine that one of them is ill and hospitalized. Now imagine that the well partner can't visit the sick one because they are of the same sex, and the law does not confer any such rights to this couple. You can call a policy that denies visitation in a case like this many things. "Pro-family" is not one of them.

We have reached a point in this country where religious conservatives will argue, in all sincerity, that policies like this should be upheld. They argue that states should have the right to deny their LGBTQ residents the right to adopt or to serve as foster parents.

We are actually at a place where some groups would rather see children with no home than in one headed by a same-sex couple.

Other conservatives have insisted that it's appropriate for the government to police the sexual behavior of adults—even as they scream about "freedom" and noninterference from the state in just about every other context. In 2013, Virginia attorney general Kenneth T. Cuccinelli II, a favorite of the religious Right, attempted to enforce the state's law prohibiting sodomy, a piece of legislation that was invalidated by the Supreme Court's ruling in 2003's *Lawrence v. Texas*. It took a ruling from a federal appeals court to stop Cuccinelli.

When you see things like this and hear augments that are this vitriolic and irrational, it's a sign that some powerful, if dark, force has been set loose.

What is it? What's going on here?

Fear. It's the fear of change and the fear of a society that will look different than the one that has existed for a long time.

It's the fear of losing "our way of life." It's the fear of a society that has chosen to expand its vision rather than restrict it.

The problem is, this fear-based argument has been raised in the face of every social change to confront this nation. And it is always wrong.

It appeared during the first waves of immigration from countries like Ireland, Italy, Poland, Russia, and China, as well as from Slavic nations, when we were told that these newcomers were changing the face of our nation.

It appeared when women sought their rights, and we were told that society wasn't ready for equality between the sexes and that emancipated women would upset God's plan for society.

It appeared when African Americans fought off Jim Crow, and we were told that the time had not yet come for racial equality.

It appeared more recently in yet another xenophobic wave of attacks on Latino immigrants, who, we were told, were remaking our nation too quickly.

It appears today in the wake of crude attacks on Muslims, who are all labeled terrorists and accused of seeking to impose sharia law on the nation.

Each of these movements share one thing in common: they challenged an entrenched power structure—entrenched but not unassailable. We have a history of overcoming the fear and becoming a stronger nation for it. Oftentimes, we look back with dismay on such bouts with hate and xenophobia and ask, "What could they have been thinking?"

What could religious conservatives be thinking now? Probably that they're about to lose the nation they consider their property. This is a groundless fear, primarily because you can't lose something that you never owned.

In March of 2013, the *Washington Post* published the results of a poll on attitudes toward same-sex marriage. The poll found that 58 percent of respondents said they favored marriage equality. Among people aged eighteen to twenty-nine, a stunning 81 percent were in favor.[12]

Bryan Fischer, a staff member at the American Family Association who has made a name for himself for employing extreme rhetoric, was not impressed.

"[Young people] don't need to be pandered to; they need to be educated," Fisher bellowed on a radio show. "We don't pander to the least mature, least intelligent, least informed, least experienced, least educated members of our movement; we educate them."[13]

Keep talking, Fischer. Fewer and fewer people are listening.

Change will come, no matter what the Catholic bishops and their religious Right allies say or do. The trend is toward more freedom and personal responsibility, not less.

Nowhere is this more desirable—and nowhere is religious interference more unwelcome—than in the realm of sexuality, the most intimate and personal of all human relationships.

4

EDUCATION

Religious conservatives can't decide what to do about public education. Sometimes they want to take over the schools and "Christianize" them; other times they want to abolish the entire system and move toward a network of private, sectarian schools funded by taxpayers through voucher plans.

Public schools are a target for the right wing, and they have been for a long time. There are two main reasons for this. One is that most children in America, about 90 percent, attend public schools. The other is that religious conservatives used to exert great influence over the schools but, in recent years, have seen that decrease; they'd like to get it back.

There are many myths about public education in America. In my travels in the world of the religious Right, I'm frequently amazed at the things I hear being said about public schools. What's even more remarkable is that many of these comments come from people who either no longer have children in the public schools or have never had them there in the first place. Nevertheless, they feel certain that they know what goes on in those institutions.

Because public schools educate so many of our young people, they are fat and juicy targets for the right wing. As I've mentioned, public education brings together two strains of right-wing thought: Religious fundamentalists view the schools as a mission field. They see them as full of "unsaved" and "unchurched" children whose parents have dared to raise them in some religious or philosophical system other than fundamentalism. They can't help but salivate at the thought of gaining access to the schools and the children within to use them as conduits for evangelism.

More secular-oriented right-wingers look at the schools and salivate too. Only they salivate over the money spent on public education. It runs in the billions. Antigovernment conservatives, with their childlike faith in the free market and hostility toward any and all public services, would love nothing better than to turn over education to corporate raiders who would be only too happy to bust teachers' unions and privatize American education.

Because public education touches the lives of so many Americans, it's the perfect vehicle for the Far Right to gain power over us—if only they can subdue it or Christianize it. Failing that, the best thing to do from their perspective would be to abolish it, lest it fall into enemy hands (which many of them believe it has. At religious Right gatherings, you still hear dark talk about "secular humanists" running the schools, straight out of 1981).

This has been a long-running battle. As with some of the other issues we've looked at in this book, a sense of history is helpful to understand better what's going on. Why do religious conservatives obsess so much over public education? Because they once controlled it, and they'd like to regain that control. It's the only way they can get back into a position to make decisions for other people's children.

Many Americans might be surprised to learn that public education hasn't always existed in the United States. Although some of our Founding Fathers supported the idea of educating the masses, the concept was slow to catch on. In a largely agrarian nation, which the United States was for a long time, many people saw little need to educate their children beyond some basics. Most likely, they were going to end up working on a farm or perhaps learning a trade.

The wealthy elite educated their children, of course, because they expected them to enter professions such as law, politics, or the ministry. The wealthy relied on private tutors. Public education didn't really start to take hold in America until after the Civil War.

Even then, it was sporadic, and there was no obligation for children to attend. Many states had no compulsory-attendance laws until well into the twentieth century.

When public schools did begin to grow, they tended to have a generically Protestant religious feel to them. This isn't surprising because most Americans were members of Protestant denominations. But the country was changing, thanks in part to immigration from heavily Catholic countries. Conflict was inevitable.

The problem wasn't just that the schools were Protestant in character; it was that this feature of the schools was used as a tool to remind non-Protestant newcomers of their second-class status. WASP-ridden America looked with great suspicion on immigrants from nations like Ireland, Italy, Poland, and the like. These largely Catholic nations were seen as producing an inferior sort of person, suitable for perhaps the lowest forms of manual labor.

The conundrum for the ruling Protestant elite sounds familiar to today's ears: it wanted cheap labor, but it didn't necessarily want to share its society with the people doing the cheap labor. Once those people were here, they were to be controlled as much as possible.

One way the Protestant upper crust kept the newcomers down was through the public schools. Catholic children didn't just have their rights violated in public schools, they were sometimes humiliated by being forced to take part in Protestant religious exercises. Those who refused faced the possibility of being punished with beatings or expelled from the schools.

A system like this could not last; challenges were inevitable, and they did come.

Many Americans today believe that controversies over prayer and Bible reading in schools are of relatively recent vintage, and they point to the Supreme Court's 1962 and 1963 rulings in this area. What they're overlooking is the body of cases that came out of state courts in the late nineteenth and early twentieth centuries.

As long as there have been public schools, people have been fighting over the role of religion in them. This is no surprise. As

I've mentioned elsewhere in this book, Americans often don't see eye to eye on religion. That's kind of the point of America. You don't have to see eye to eye. You have the right to believe what you want, to worship as you please, and to pass those views on to your offspring. But when your religion starts to affect the rights of someone else, there will be conflict.

Problems also occur when arms of the government start taking sides on theological disputes. For a long time, that's exactly what the public-school system did in America—it took sides on matters of theology.

In many states in the nineteenth century, the school day began with the recitation of the Lord's Prayer and the reading of some set number of verses of the Bible without comment. Those two words—*without comment*—are significant. In some states, they even appeared in laws dealing with the role of religion in public schools.[1]

Early advocates of public education—Massachusetts politician and education reformer Horace Mann among them—wanted to find a way to defuse some of the battles over religion in schools. Mann and others believed the Bible could be used in public schools in a way that would highlight its moral lessons without getting into sectarian questions. They viewed reading Bible verses in school "without comment" as one way to do this.

What they failed to grasp is that this practice is in itself sectarian. Generally speaking, most Protestant sects stress the right of the individual believer to interpret scripture as guided by his or her conscience. Some denominations, like many Baptists, heavily stress this point and believe that each person has the right to approach God on his or her own terms, without the need of intermediaries.

This is not a view shared by most Catholics. Certainly Catholics believe in approaching God directly through prayer, but they are also much more likely to turn to clergy for advice and help in interpreting biblical passages. Thus, reading Bible verses without comment was really a Protestant practice. (The fact that Catholics and Protestants use different versions of the Bible and that the version used in the public schools was always the Protestant one was another complicating factor.)

Of course, the use of the Bible and only the Bible excluded Jews, nonbelievers, and members of other faiths. The fight over religion in public schools tends to be looked at through the lens of the Protestant/Catholic divide that was so prominent at this time, but it's a mistake to see it exclusively through these terms.

The late nineteenth century saw the rise of a vigorous and spirited nontheistic movement in the United States. These early free-thinkers, led by men like Robert G. Ingersoll, known as "the Great Agnostic," criticized the morality of the Bible and challenged the veracity of the accounts found within it. Ingersoll and his allies would not have agreed with reading biblical passages in schools without comment either. They would rather the Bible not be used devotionally in public schools at all.

Inevitably, this issue went to court. As I noted, the early cases were fought in state courts. The most prominent case occurred in Cincinnati in the late 1860s and resulted in an 1872 ruling from the Ohio Supreme Court stating that education officials in that city had the right to end school-sponsored Bible readings in the schools.[2]

This incident is known today as the "Cincinnati Bible War," and *war* is not too strong a word to use. It can be difficult for us today to grasp how strongly people felt about these issues. Sometimes they took to the streets. In Philadelphia, a riot that lasted several days broke out in 1844 after word spread that the school board planned to end Bible reading in the public schools. The rumor wasn't even true. In fact, the school board was merely looking at some options to excuse Catholic children from the religious exercises, but even that was enough to spark violence, causing several deaths and the destruction of a handful of buildings.[3]

Obviously there was a lot going on in the country at that time, and tensions over religion in public schools were in some ways just a visible manifestation of underlying conflict. As I've noted, the waves of immigration in the middle of the nineteenth century roiled the nation and sparked social conflict. Immigrants from heavily Catholic nations were seen as suspicious foreigners with their own rituals, possibly holding a loyalty chiefly to the Vatican. Wild stories spread about secret plans to make America officially Catholic and subservient to the pope in Rome. Americans would be forced to bend to church law. In some ways, it was similar to claims we hear today that Muslims seek to impose Islamic law on America.

But there is an additional component about the nineteenth-century battle that is sometimes overlooked or downplayed: the Catholic Church at that time did not recognize separation of church and state. The church's view was that governments did have an obligation to submit to church fathers. Clearly this was not going to happen in the United States, which had a large Protestant majority, but Americans did not have to look far to see nations that were under the de facto control of the church. Obviously Protestants in America overreacted, but Catholic Church officials, at times, did their cause little favor with their rhetoric.

The problem is that Protestants of the day tended to raise a separation-of-church-and-state argument when they didn't really mean it. What many conservative Protestants in the nineteenth century wanted was not church-state separation but the ability to continue controlling society as much as possible through public institutions like the schools. It wasn't until the modern era that many religious leaders began to flesh out a more honest interpretation of separation of church and state as a principle that applied to all groups and gave none undue influence over public schools.

For proof of this, we look at only the reaction to the Supreme Court's rulings concerning school prayer in the 1960s. In the wake of these rulings, there was widespread condemnation among conservative religious groups, both Protestant and Catholic. In other words, by the 1960s, secularism was seen as a greater threat than Protestant/Catholic squabbling.

Liberal and moderate religious leaders held a more nuanced view. To them, the loss of school prayer was no big deal; in fact, they welcomed its demise. They pointed out that the prayers were imposed by the state, that they were coercive, and that undoubtedly many young people simply mumbled their way through them every morning without stopping to think about what they were even saying. These by-rote religious exercises were hardly meaningful in a spiritual sense and did little to bring youngsters closer to God or a genuine faith.

Considering how empty official school prayers and Bible readings were from a spiritual standpoint, it's amazing that so many religious conservatives went to the mat so often to save these exercises. Yet they did, over and over again. Many of them even supported constitutional amendments to "restore" school prayer, and they continue such efforts to this day.

Something else was going on here. In time, it would become obvious that the battles over school prayer in the 1960s were early rumblings in the culture wars that would erupt with such fervor in the 1980s. These battles were also evidence that religious conservatives were not going to loosen their grip over public education. They intended to go down fighting.

The 1960s were a period of social and cultural upheaval. They were also a time of liberation movements. 1964 saw the passage of the landmark Civil Rights Act. Federal forces intervened in Southern states to safeguard the right to vote. Women stepped up their push for equality. The nation even saw the beginnings of the gay-rights movement with the Stonewall riots in 1969.

For some Americans, most religious conservatives among them, this was simply too much too soon. The pace of social change had hit light speed, and it was time to slow things down. Not surprisingly, religious conservatives—Protestant and Catholic—banded together to build a backlash.

When societies move through periods of difficult cultural change, religious conservatives almost always react with a cry to return to old ways, which they label something like *traditional values*. Terms like this are euphemisms. *Traditional* sounds nice.

Who could be against tradition? We honor our traditions, after all. And *values* are very positive. What's the alternative—having no values?

The creation of this term was a kind of a public-relations masterstroke. What religious conservatives really wanted was their power back. They wanted to be able to call the shots in public education, as they had done for so long. They wanted to be able to tell others what to do, to be the boss of us. But saying that would have caused people to recoil. Calling for "traditional values" sounded much less threatening.

Liberals and moderates who peeked behind the curtain would see what those "values" were: women back in the home or limited to clerical or support-staff jobs; the suppression of anything seen as "un-American" and the elevation of a type of national "civil religion" that just happened to reflect right-wing theology of one God who loved America the best.

Disturbed by this agenda, liberals and moderates sounded the alarm. The early skirmishes are familiar to anyone who lived through the late 1970s and the Reagan presidency that followed: Anita Bryant's war against gays in Florida, charges that public-school textbooks promoted "secular humanism," attacks on rock music and youth culture. (See more on this in the chapter on culture.)

Demands that public schools reflect a Christian ethos were part of this drive. During the 1980 campaign, Ronald Reagan courted religious conservatives aggressively and vowed to enact a school-prayer amendment, if elected. Once in office, Reagan did indeed have the amendment introduced, and it even faced a vote in the Senate, where it failed to garner the necessary two-thirds vote.

At the same time, religious Right activists reignited their war on modern science. Fundamentalists had been sparring with evolution since the 1920s and the famous Scopes trial in Tennessee. Popular mythology holds that fundamentalists were so humiliated in that case, they ran home with their tails between their legs and hid under their beds for several decades.

The truth is a little more complex. People tend to forget that the teacher in the case, John Scopes, was found guilty of teaching evolution, although his conviction was later overturned on a technicality. Scopes's attorney, the famous crusader Clarence Darrow, did indeed make fundamentalists—including opposing attorney William Jennings Bryan—look foolish.

But the Scopes trial was hardly a rout for evolution. Many public schools still avoided the subject, and it wasn't until the 1950s, when the Soviet Union appeared to be pulling ahead in satellite technology, that a renewed emphasis on science boosted evolution in the classrooms.

Even that did not last. By the 1970s, many states were once again looking for ways to water down the teaching of evolution. Religious fundamentalists, always keen to cover their tracks with euphemisms, began promoting "creation science"—essentially, biblical fundamentalism masquerading as a type of science.

Creation science had a few drawbacks. Chiefly, it wasn't science. Its foundational claims—that the Earth is only six thousand years old and that humans coexisted with dinosaurs—are absurd. It also violated a cardinal rule of science: it started with an answer and worked backward, not with a question and pushed forward. Creation science had no peer-reviewed journals and was not taught in secular universities, although it was popular in fundamentalist Bible colleges.

Advocates of creation science had a disturbing tendency to employ nonscientific arguments. For example, when challenged with the voluminous fossil evidence in favor of an ancient planet that underscores the reality of evolution, some of them gamely replied that Satan could have easily put those fossils there to trip us up or that the world was created to appear ancient as a test of faith.

Despite the paucity of their arguments, creationists were soon running amok and laying waste to science education in several states. Legislators in Louisiana went so far as to pass a law mandating that creation science be taught alongside evolution in public schools. The Supreme Court struck down this so-called balanced-treatment law in 1987.[4]

Religious fundamentalists reconvened and pushed ahead. Some of them began using the term *creationism* instead, as if to admit that the game was up and this thing they so favored was not science. Others latched onto even more creative terms—*the theory of abrupt appearance* and *evidence against evolution* became popular favorites.

Then came *intelligent design* (ID). Again, it was a masterstroke of a euphemism. We humans look pretty complex, and we're so jammed full of working parts (well, most of them work; the appendix is an exception), that who wouldn't want to think that some intelligent force assembled us?

Plus, intelligent design gave creationists the power to jettison some of the more ridiculous claims about the age of the planet and focus instead on questions that, on the surface, at least, sounded like real science: How could this especially complex part of us have evolved? Real scientists then took the time to explain how this especially complex part of us did evolve, but by then, the IDers were on to something else.

The real genius of ID is that it claims to be secular and thus appropriate for use in public schools. Intelligent-design advocates insist that they haven't identified the designer. Sure, it could be the Christian God, but it doesn't have to be.

Unfortunately, for ID proponents, other than the Christian God, they are low on possible designer candidates. Space aliens have been mentioned, as have time travelers who came back (most likely in a DeLorean) and seeded life. Of course, this raises the question of who intelligently designed the space aliens or the time travelers. Presumably, this is the sort of thing youngsters could explore during ID science fairs.

Intelligent design ran into a bit of a problem in 2005, when a federal court in Pennsylvania ruled that it was just warmed-over creationism and ejected it from public schools in the town of Dover.[5] Residents of that small community had endured the antics of a school board determined to keep evil Darwinian ideas out of the classroom—even though the science teachers in the district were more than happy to invite Mr. Darwin in. In response to the court case challenging ID, the voters had their revenge. They went to the polls and ejected the pro-ID slate from the board.

The entire sorry situation over creationism is an example of one of the most tragic effects of religious conservatives' determination to run the lives of others: the spread of ignorance and scientific illiteracy across the nation.

Creationists and their ID cousins simply don't know or don't care what science is. Their main concern seems to be that Darwin's theory somehow removes God from the equation. God is more important than Darwin; therefore, Darwin must go. The two aren't compatible.

Of course, for many religious people, God and Darwin *are* compatible. This is one area, for example, where the leadership of the Catholic Church breaks with fundamentalist Protestants. A stray bishop here and there may flirt with intelligent design, but the hierarchy's official line is that one need not reject Darwin's theory to embrace God. Evolution, the bishops say, could be an instrument of the divinity.

Some may scoff at this. That's their right, although I think it's shortsighted. Nonbelievers and those who insist that science has made faith obsolete should be careful. The United States remains a highly religious country. If people are told that they can't have both religion and science and that they must choose one, most will go with religion and shut out science. This shutting out is much to the detriment of our young people.

Fundamentalists have been successful by portraying the conflict as a stark choice between God and Darwin. It's a false choice, but they keep thrusting it in our faces. The reality is that one can have both. The bishops have looked at the evidence, seen that it is overwhelmingly in favor of evolution, and sought to find a way to reconcile faith and science.

Consider the case of the Catholic Church, an institution that has been around for two thousand years and has a long memory: some prior incidents where faith and science clashed that didn't work out so well for faith—Galileo, call your office!—may have influenced its decision to be more flexible this time around. In other words, the leaders of the Catholic Church don't want to be on the wrong side of science again. They've been burned before.

Fundamentalist Protestants aren't there yet—and they may never be. Their problem is that they persist in looking at the Bible as a science book. It's not. This should be pretty obvious to anyone who reads it. The Bible is a collection of works cobbled together by people who lived thousands of years ago. It reflects a prescientific understanding of the world. This is not to imply that it has no value, only that is must be looked at in light of the times that produced it. We can no more expect accurate science from the Bible than we can expect to find the genetic code outlined in the writings of Hippocrates.

Yet we find ourselves in this curious position: in an age where people in supersonic jets fly around the globe in hours and communicate instantly at the speed of light, at a time of antibiotics and gene therapy, during a period of space travel and robotics, religious fundamentalists insist that a book written by desert nomads thousands of years ago contains a more accurate depiction of human origins than works produced by PhD biologists at a major research university. And they have convinced many Americans to agree with them.

This is the ultimate tragedy of creationism. How many children have been turned away from careers in science because they were not taught real science in school? How far is our nation lagging behind countries like China and India because biology teachers have been so browbeaten that some of them won't even use the term *evolution* in class?

I mentioned that the state of Louisiana once passed a law mandating the teaching of creationism alongside evolution in public schools, a measure that was struck down by the Supreme Court. Sadly, Louisiana legislators learned nothing from that experience.

In 2008, Louisiana lawmakers passed a so-called Science Education Act that allows teachers to use "supplemental" materials in class. These materials, to no one's surprise, undermine evolution and promote creationist ideas. Science educators at the state's leading universities opposed the bill but to no avail. It sailed through the legislature and became law.

What has this law done for Louisiana? Who seriously looks at that state as a font of cutting-edge science? Instead, Louisiana is too often seen as a backwater. By elevating fundamentalism over actual science, Louisiana lawmakers signaled that they don't mind leaving their young people behind.

State lawmakers portrayed this as matter of religious freedom. This argument has surfaced in other states. The argument is made that no student should have to learn things that conflict with his or her faith.

The problem with that argument is that what is being promoted is not religious freedom—it's the freedom to be ignorant. Everyone has the right to be ignorant, of course. In America, a person can believe that the Earth is the center of the universe and that a race of dog-people from Pluto traveled through space to build the pyramids.

Yet the right to believe nonsense or that which is demonstrably untrue is not something the state should celebrate or facilitate. The purpose of public education is not to foster the right to be ignorant; it is to combat it and to show that there is a better way. I've mentioned several times the idea that a public good can trump an extreme individual interpretation of religious freedom. Efforts to make all children ignorant by denying them instruction about modern science must be opposed and stopped because they do not foster the public good. Americans have the right to teach their children whatever they like at home—even pernicious nonsense. I wish they wouldn't do that, but they have the right. They don't have the right to use a bogus religious-freedom argument to insert pernicious nonsense into the public-school curriculum.

We've been to this place before; it is not a good place to be. Consider previous attempts to warp science to meet the demands of fundamentalist interpretations of the Bible, such as flat-Earth concepts.

Advocates of ID and other forms of creationism get angry when someone brings up the flat Earth. How dare anyone compare their ideas to such obvious tomfoolery? What they don't want to admit is that it wasn't so long ago that fundamentalists were citing the Bible to buttress flat-Earth ideas, pointing to passages in Genesis, Daniel, Psalms, and other books. Such beliefs were held by some fundamentalists into the twentieth century. Until the 1930s, in Zion, Illinois, a community founded by a strict fundamentalist sect that was a quasi theocracy, schools taught that the Earth is flat.[6]

There are some fundamentalists today who cling to equally discredited ideas because the Bible tells them to. A few years ago, after I appeared on CNN to battle with a religious Right activist over the issue of creationism, I received a letter and a book from a gentleman named Gerardus D. Bouw, PhD, who wanted me to know that the Earth is the center of the universe and that it does not move. Bouw directed me to a site advocating these ideas—"geocentricity"—which he insisted is fully supported by the Bible. At the geocentricity site (www.geocentricity.com), you will see a link to the "Galileo Was Wrong" site right above the official Statement of Faith of the Association for Biblical Astronomy.

The latter includes the "Credo of the Biblical Astronomer," which reads, in part, "We believe that the creation was completed in six twenty-four hour days and that the world is not older than about six thousand years. We maintain that the Bible teaches us of an earth that neither rotates daily nor revolves yearly about the sun; that it is at rest with respect to the throne of him who called it into existence; and that hence it is absolutely at rest in the universe."[7] (I assure you that I was not taken in by *The Onion*. In fact, I was so startled by this material that I called my friend Glenn Branch at the National Center for Science Education just to make certain I was not being hoaxed. Branch assured me that Bouw really means it.)

Today, we can laugh at the promotion of such obviously discredited ideas that the Earth is stagnant and so young. Yet creationists belong in the same camp; they just have more popular support (in America at least—they get little traction elsewhere in the Western world).

We should never mistake what religious conservatives are trying to do. To them, it's never enough to be able to teach their own children the tenets of their faith and elevate their interpretation of a book they deem holy over modern science. They want to drag everyone else's kids into the Dark Ages with them.

This mind-set manifests itself in many ways in public education. To my mind, it is the heart and soul of the culture wars that plague our public schools.

Consider this: Parents have the right to instruct their children on how to pray. Those children can then pray in school, as long as they do not do so in a disruptive manner. Under a federal law called the Equal Access Act, secondary-school students can, under most circumstances, form voluntary religious clubs during noninstructional time and meet with their likeminded friends for prayer and the reading of religious texts.

It would seem that there is plenty of opportunity for religious worship in public schools for those who want it. Why isn't this enough?

It isn't enough because, to many fundamentalists, religious freedom—that is, the right of an individual to engage in prayer or other religious acts—isn't really what they want. They seek the right to use government channels to impose their faith on others.

I'm no theologian, but even I know that Jesus warned his followers not to make a big public show of their prayers. Such displays, Jesus said, were something hypocrites did. Christ advised praying in secret and told his followers that God would know of their prayers and reward them (see Matthew 6:5–6).

Followers of the religious Right have taken this rather clear admonition and turned it completely on its head. To them, it seems as if a prayer doesn't even count unless it's shouted in unison before a public event or everyone is made to acknowledge it during a meeting of the city council. To them, prayer is a type of weapon used to show other people who's in control.

Worse yet are the people who wish to use public forums to engage in sermons. There is a place for sermons—in church. A public high-school graduation ceremony, an event that is honoring young people of many faith traditions and of none, is not that place. Believe it or not, some people just want to attend a government-run event without hearing a sermon.

Religious Right groups scream that religious freedom is violated when students are told to curb the sermonizing during public school events. It's not. Religious freedom would be violated if the government attempted to stop someone from offering a sermon in a house of worship or even in a public space like a town green or a sidewalk that's recognized as an open forum. No one has the right to insist that the government provide them with a forum for spreading their faith, and, in the case of graduation speeches, school officials routinely screen student talks to make sure the speaker doesn't stray off topic.

We have come to a strange place in this country. For years, churches not only survived but also thrived by going their own way. The variety of denominations in this country is stunning. They run the gamut from liberal to conservative and include not just every conceivable variety of Christianity but also Judaism, Islam, Hinduism, Buddhism, Shintoism, Paganism, Wicca, New Age religions, and so on.

Every one of these groups built themselves up from the ground. Now we are told that they somehow cannot survive unless they are able to use government channels, like the public schools, to broadcast their messages and seek new converts.

I should be fair to the vast majority of religious groups in America by pointing out that this is almost always a fundamentalist-Christian phenomenon. They are the ones who constantly seek to infiltrate the public schools, often through the use of deceit and ruses.

For example, fundamentalist groups sponsor a variety of motivational speakers, self-appointed experts on topics like drugs and suicide, and rock bands that roam the country, offering free or cheap assemblies to public schools. Any principal foolish enough to say yes to this soon finds out what's really going on: it's all a ploy to preach fundamentalism to young people. The speaker who claims to know so much about drugs may offer some basic information before lapsing into the real reason for the visit: to say that Jesus is the answer.

I've worked to defend separation of church and state for more than a quarter of a century. I've encountered this stunt time and time again. And when I do, it is always fundamentalist Christians who are behind it. Every time. I've yet to encounter a roving band of Unitarians who sneak into public schools so they can preach to kids about the inherent worth and dignity of every person.

When I hear about things like this—that involve actual deception and lies—I have to wonder what's going on. It's as if fundamentalist groups have lost faith in their ability to spread their message through voluntary channels. Let's face it, these groups have no shortage of microphones. Their TV ministries fill the airwaves, they own thousands of radio stations, and they control huge publishing arms. They are well represented in cyberspace and are usually pretty quick to exploit any new medium to spread the word of God.

And yet some people have not responded to them. Instead of accepting the fact that some people don't like their message and that those people are comfortable with their own religion or philosophy, thank you very much, fundamentalist groups all too often insist that they have a right to use a public institution, especially the public-school system, to proselytize. They assert that the failure to give them control of this forum is a type of persecution.

The greatest irony is that although they frame their argument in terms of religious freedom, they would extend that freedom to no other group, especially one they consider a rival for the hearts and minds (and souls) of young people.

Let's say a school-prayer amendment passed tomorrow, and

public school officials could once again lead children in group prayer. Now imagine that a teacher somewhere starts the prayer with these words, "Let the Goddess bless us everyone—straight, gay, bisexual, and transgendered. Let the Goddess bless the conservatives and the liberals. Goddess, please bless the Christians, the Jews, the Pagans, and all others. Blessed be."

Or imagine a prayer beginning, "In the name of Allah, the compassionate and the merciful." Or perhaps, "We'll begin today with a reading from the works of L. Ron Hubbard."

For years, fundamentalists dismissed scenarios like this because they were confident their numbers would always be strong enough to overwhelm the competition. I would not be so sure of it these days. Protestants now account for slightly less than 50 percent of the population, and the number of "nones," those who say they have no religion, keeps rising.

My point is, what religious conservatives want in public schools is not religious freedom. It is religious freedom *for them*. And what they call freedom is the power to control others. They cloak their desire to control and direct the religious lives of others in the noble garment of religious freedom, but no one should be fooled. True advocates for religious freedom stand up for the rights of everyone, not just their own kind.

Some people in the religious Right are so frustrated over their inability to infuse public education with fundamentalist Christianity that they have called for pulling the plug on the entire system. They're advocating a system of private, mostly religious schools instead.

Once again this is framed as religious freedom. Americans should have the right, they argue, to send their children to religious schools.

The problem is, there's no controversy here. Americans already have the right to send their children to private schools. This right has been secure at least since 1925, when the Supreme Court struck down an Oregon law, passed by ballot initiative, that required just about all children in the state to attend public schools.[8]

The government provides no barriers to private-school admission. Private schools in the United States, especially religious ones, are largely unregulated. They get to determine their own curriculum and make their own decisions about hiring staff. In some states, they might be subjected to minimal health and safety regulations, but, by and large, they are left alone.

It would seem to be a good arrangement. But, again, it's not enough for some religious conservatives. They are now arguing that their alleged religious-freedom right to send their children to private institutions is meaningless unless the government helps them pay for it. Their solution is education vouchers.

The Catholic bishops came up with this argument years ago. Catholics schools, they asserted, were out of reach financially for some parents, thus the government has an obligation to help out.

It's a remarkable argument, coming as it does from one of the wealthiest churches in the world. The Catholic Church runs a private-school system because it prefers education that reflects its dogma. No one would dispute its right to do this. Many do dispute its insistence that it be permitted to hand the bill for these schools to the taxpayer.

If the church hierarchy really believes that Catholic education is essential, it could fund scholarships for low-income families, seek money from private foundations, or engage in other projects to make the schools affordable. It failed to do this, and over the years, many Catholic parents realized there was no need to divert money to pay for Catholic schooling when there were perfectly good public schools in the community, especially when many parents would rather focus on saving for the ever-increasing cost of a college education. As a result, Catholic-school enrollment has dropped, and many schools have had to close.

Normally, conservatives would look at a situation like this and conclude that market forces were at work. The Catholic Church offered a product, education, but there were too few buyers, so the market responded and some schools closed. It's kind of like how cell phones muscled out pagers. In this case, they argued instead that the government should bail out Catholic schools by forcing the taxpayer to subsidize these institutions.

The bishops don't try to pretend that their schools serve any secular purpose. Although many Catholic schools accept non-Catholic pupils, they are under no obligation to do so. A Catholic school can expel a non-Catholic student if a Catholic family wants the slot. Also, these schools routinely require all students—Catholic and non-Catholic—to take part in Catholic worship.

Catholic schools (and many other sectarian educational institutions) also impose religious qualifications on the people they hire. Teachers in Catholic schools have been fired for getting divorced, being gay, supporting gay rights, getting pregnant outside wedlock, or running afoul of other church tenets.

Church leaders also boast about how their schools serve the church's ends and are used as instruments of evangelism. Christian-fundamentalist academies are notorious for saturating every class—even math—with dogma. Catholic schools do less of this, but it's no secret that the bishops see their school system first and foremost as a vehicle to strengthen the faith and project it onto others. That's fine—but it's obviously a sectarian goal and is something that Catholics should pay for, not all taxpayers.

Few would challenge the church's right to run its schools as the bishops see fit. It's their school system, after all. What bothers many people is that church leaders want to retain absolute control over their schools while demanding that the taxpayers support them. Once again, church officials want all the public support they can get but none of the oversight. The fact that they are issuing these demands in the name of religious freedom is especially audacious.

The organization I work for, Americans United for Separation of Church and State, has many disagreements with the voucher plan. Promises are often made that don't come to pass. In states with vouchers, for example, no independent studies have shown a boost in student academic performance. The scheme also appears to be a way to break the back of teachers' unions and move toward privatization of secondary education, which would allow corporate interests to move in and do what they do best: offer the cheapest product possible to maximize profits and keep stockholders happy. That might be a nice formula for making snow tires; it would be a disaster when applied to education. Some things are more important than profit. Educating our children is one of them.

And in some states, voucher proponents openly try to exclude religious schools they don't like from these plans. In Tennessee, a voucher bill had been on the fast track to pass in 2013 but was slowed down when someone pointed out that Muslim schools might seek to take part. Legislators actually went back to the drawing board to look for ways to exclude these schools.

Of course there is no such way. And, in fact, the conundrum in Tennessee underscores the problem with vouchers: people don't want to pay for a religion that is not their own.

The main objection to vouchers and other attempts to shift education from the public sector to the private/religious one will always rest on separation of church and state. Put simply, everyone has a religious-freedom right to patronize sectarian education if they choose, but no one has a right under religious freedom to make you pay for the propagation of their faith.

Likewise, no one has the right to use a system of public education designed to serve us all and turn it into a vehicle to proselytize for their own faith. If your religious freedom needs a boost so badly that the only way you can get people to pay attention to your faith is by hijacking captive audiences through a government apparatus, take a look at what you're doing. Chances are it's not religious freedom at all.

5

POLITICS

T he interaction of religion and politics raises two issues, one relatively straightforward and one more nuanced.

The straightforward issue concerns what United States law says about nonprofit organizations and how they may intervene in politics. The more nuanced issue raises questions of how religious groups can speak to political leaders and advocate for their ideas in a democratic, pluralistic society that places a premium on individual rights and self-determination.

We'll begin with what the law says. First off, nothing in the law prevents religious groups from advocating for their positions in the political arena. Houses of worship, like any other interest group, have the right to speak out. There is a long history of this in the United States. Over the years, churches have been all over the map on any number of political controversies.

Religious Right activists are fond of pointing out that some clergy during the colonial period supported the call for revolution. This is certainly true; some did. Others took the opposite view. The implication by the religious Right is that this long record of political intervention by members of the clergy somehow validates political activity being undertaken today by the politicized clergy of the religious Right. It's a strange argument.

As usual, the religious Right fails to get the point. Complaints are raised over church involvement in politics not because the church is involved; it's because of what the church is trying to achieve. Few Americans seriously expect houses of worship to be entirely apolitical. All Americans are asking is that churches play by some basic ground rules.

In the United States, those rules are clear: nonprofit organizations may not use tax-exempt resources to endorse or oppose candidates for public office. Note that this rule is limited to candidates, not issues. The thinking is that nonprofit status, which is a very desirable benefit extended to groups that are supposedly operating in the public interest, should not be abused. In other words, a nonprofit group can't expect to behave like a political action committee (PAC) and get away with it.

Religious Right groups don't see it this way. To them, the restriction on partisan endorsements of candidates is a violation of free speech and religious freedom. They overlook one salient point: no one is forcing them to be tax exempt. A house of worship that seeks to intervene in partisan politics by endorsing or opposing candidates has the option to surrender its tax exemption. They never want to do this.

Once again, we see an instance where powerful churches want (and, in fact, *demand*) a lucrative government benefit and then insist that they don't want to follow the rules that come with said government benefit.

The simple truth is that tax exemption comes with a number of conditions. How could it be any other way? The Internal Revenue Service (IRS) must have some way of policing tax exemption, or the concept would be abused by sham organizations that simply don't want to pay taxes.

Generally speaking, most organizations in the United States that are tax exempt operate under Section 501 (c)(3) of the Internal Revenue Code. You might have heard people speak of "(c)(3) groups"—this is just another way of saying "tax exempt."

Groups designated as 501 (c)(3) come in many varieties. Examples are environmental organizations, animal-welfare groups, organizations that promote medical research, museums, educational institutions, and assorted advocacy groups. This category also includes houses of worship and ministries.

These groups share certain features. The idea is that they exist not to generate profit (as a corporation does) but to serve the public good. They are freed from taxation while they pursue this goal. In addition, the donations people make to these organizations are tax deductible (for those who itemize their taxes).

The ban on overt partisan politicking is just one rule tax-exempt groups must follow. There are many others. For example, a group that raises money from the public to address a certain issue is (not surprisingly) expected to spend most of its budget on that issue.

"Private inurement" is also prohibited. Inurement is a concept that states that the individuals who are employed or associated with nonprofit organizations may not receive "excessive compensation" or lavish benefits from these groups. Again, this is because the money raised is supposed to go toward the cause espoused by the nonprofit and not toward lining the pockets of an executive.

We've all heard stories about sham nonprofits. Years ago, I saw a story on the television newsmagazine *60 Minutes* about an alleged cancer charity that was, in fact, diverting most of the money it raised to pay the high salaries of the group's executives. Very little money was spent on cancer research.

The IRS and other government agencies will crack down on abuses like this. They have the right to do so because these nonprofit groups, by accepting 501 (c)(3) status, open themselves up to regulation and oversight. It's part of the deal.

Such intrusions by the government would likely not be accepted in the corporate world. We've all read about the excessive compensation awarded to the CEOs of some corporations. There is little the government can do about this because the entities in question are not open to intense government regulation in this area of their operations.

But nonprofits are. Again, no group is forced to accept this status. It is avidly sought because it's a powerful benefit. Many people believe that nonprofit status is a type of "seal of approval." They feel safe donating money to (c)(3) groups, believing that, since they are subject to oversight by the IRS, the groups must be on the up-and-up.

My point is that houses of worship, by actively accepting nonprofit status, have also agreed to accept a reasonable number of regulations. One of these regulations prohibits intervention in political campaigns between individuals. Churches could be free of this regulation by declining tax-exempt status. Instead, some religious leaders seek to have it both ways—they want the benefit but not the oversight. It doesn't work that way. (This is not the view of most members of the clergy. The majority of religious leaders in the United States understand the rules and follow them.)

What's even more frustrating to many observers of this issue is that houses of worship are already treated preferentially by the IRS in this area. For example, houses of worship are granted tax-exempt status by mere dint of their existence. They are not required to apply for it. They are assumed to have it as soon as they form.

That's not the case with secular nonprofits. Secular (c)(3) groups must fill out paperwork and apply for tax-exempt status. It can be a laborious process. And, of course, tax-exempt status can be denied if the group seeking it fails to make the case that it deserves it.

The IRS also more aggressively enforces some portions of the tax code against secular nonprofits. Recall the phony cancer charity that overpaid its executives; the IRS will step in and put a stop to things like that (and rightly so). This has rarely—if ever—happened to a church. A minister's compensation package simply is not questioned by the IRS.

Consider some of the TV preachers who operate in America. We've all seen and read the exposés on the way they live. Some of them are paid millions annually. They own several mansions, private jets, fleets of fancy cars, and so on. They charge daily living expenses to their ministries.

Violations like this would bring down a secular nonprofit in short order. The IRS turns away when it's a megachurch or a television ministry.

Government officials rarely even look at this stuff. On the rare occasion when they do, the religious Right is quick to holler about religious freedom. In 2007, US senator Charles Grassley (R-Iowa) asked several large TV ministries and megachurches to provide some basic financial information. Grassley was concerned that these ministries were abusing tax-exempt status. The ministries balked, although a few did eventually provide the information. Others hired attorneys and flatly refused to cooperate.[1]

In the end, the inquiry went nowhere. But even if Grassley had compiled damning information, he could not have forced the IRS to act. Sure, as a US senator, he had the power to lean on the agency in a way that you and I would not have, but even that would not have guaranteed IRS action.

Conservative religious groups, backed by religious Right legal groups, are increasingly insisting that they are beyond the reach of the IRS. The scope of their activities and arguments can be audacious.

During the 1990s, some right-wing churches began openly challenging the IRS's "no partisan politicking" rule. (Remember, this rule applies only to intervention in electoral contests between individuals; it does not prohibit speaking out on issues.) In October of 1992, a church near Binghamton, New York, actually placed full-page ads in *USA Today* and the *Washington Times* asserting that voting for Bill Clinton was a sin. The church listed several Bible passages that Clinton was allegedly in violation of.

My organization, Americans United for Separation of Church and State, was taken aback by the audacity of the move. The church must have known this was illegal. Sure enough, its leaders did. The church in question, known at the time as the Church at Pierce Creek, was active in the antiabortion movement and had ties to Randall Terry, a strident opponent of legal abortion. The ad was undoubtedly a type of test to see if the IRS would act.

In this case, the IRS did act. Responding to a complaint filed by Americans United, the tax agency pulled the church's tax-exempt status. The church duly filed a lawsuit to get it back. In court, the church was represented by TV preacher Pat Robertson's American Center for Law and Justice (ACLJ). They raised both a free-speech and a freedom-of-religion argument.

The Church at Pierce Creek lost the case in court. A federal district court initially ruled against the church, and a three-judge appellate panel later unanimously upheld the ruling.[2] Responding to the ACLJ's assertion that the IRS had no authority over the church, the court wrote, "We find this argument more creative than persuasive."

This should have settled the matter. Incredibly, it had the opposite effect. Within a few years, a religious Right legal group called the Alliance Defense Fund (ADF, which has since changed its name to the Alliance Defending Freedom) began actively urging pastors to openly violate federal law by endorsing or opposing candidates from the pulpit. Ignoring the Church at Pierce Creek case, the ADF insists that pastors have a free-speech and freedom-of-religion right to tell congregants whom to vote for or against.

Every year, the ADF sponsors an event called "Pulpit Freedom Sunday," during which pastors break the IRS rule. It's difficult to tell what exactly is going on in many of these churches. Some of the pastors merely discuss political issues, which is permitted. But with others, there is no doubt: candidates are endorsed or opposed.

Americans United has reported several of these churches to the IRS. Although the IRS continues to insist that it will enforce this law, we are unaware of any attempt at aggressive enforcement. Apparently, a few pastors have been warned—a mere slap on the wrist. The IRS conducts its investigations under strict confidentiality rules, and thus its investigations aren't usually made public.

The cases Americans United reports don't fall into a gray area. In many cases, the pastors know they are violating the law, and they don't care. A few examples bear this out.

In May of 2012, Reverend Charles L. Worley of Providence Road Baptist Church in Maiden, North Carolina, delivered a sermon insisting that God disapproves of homosexuality. He even called for gay people to be placed behind electrified fences in concentration camps and allowed to die out.

It's nasty, but so far it's protected speech. But Worley didn't stop there. He went on to attack President Barack Obama for his support of LGBTQ rights and marriage equality.

"Of our president getting up and saying that it's all right for two women to marry or two men to marry," Worley said, "I tell you right now I was disappointed bad. But I tell you right there that's as sorry as you get. The Bible's agin it, God's agin it, I'm agin it and if you've got any sense, you're agin it. . . . Somebody said, 'who you gonna vote for?' I ain't gonna vote for a baby killer and a homosexual lover. You said, 'did you mean that?' You better believe I did."[3]

Around the same time, Pastor Ronnie Spriggs of Hager Hill Freewill Baptist Church in Kentucky also attacked Obama from the pulpit.

"You can say 'that's political' if you want to and blame me if you want to, but I heard our president say something this week that I never thought I'd ever hear a president of the United States say," Spriggs said. "Did y'all hear that? He said that he believes that gays ought to have the right to marry in the United States. That's the president of the United States who said that. Amen. I don't know about you folks, but I'm going on record, and I don't care who knows it. I want the guy out. . . . This country can't afford that kind of ideology in that office. I want you to speak up in these next few months that are to come, and let's not back this kind of ideology. Let's get this out of the White House."[4]

This type of extreme rhetoric isn't limited to Protestant-fundamentalist churches. In Peoria, Illinois, Bishop Daniel R. Jenky of the Catholic diocese blasted Obama for supporting wider access to birth control. Jenky compared Obama to Joseph Stalin and Adolf Hitler.

"Hitler and Stalin, at their better moments, would just barely tolerate some churches remaining open, but would not tolerate any competition with the state in education, social services, and health care," Jenky said during an April 2012 sermon. "In clear violation of our First Amendment rights, Barack Obama—with his radical, pro-abortion and extreme secularist agenda, now seems intent on following a similar path." Now things have come to such a pass in America that this is a battle that we could lose, but before the awesome judgment seat of Almighty God this is not a war where any believing Catholic may remain neutral.[5]

Jenky added, "This fall, every practicing Catholic must vote, and must vote their Catholic consciences, or by the following fall our Catholic schools, our Catholic hospitals, our Catholic Newman Centers, all our public ministries—only excepting our church buildings—could easily be shut down."[6]

Shortly before the election, Jenky struck again. He issued a pastoral letter to church members asserting that anyone who voted for candidates who support reproductive rights would face "God's perfect judgment."[7]

Jenky wasn't the only one issuing such letter. Just days before the election, Bishop David L. Ricken of Green Bay, Wisconsin, decided to offer his flock some advice. In a nutshell, it was this: voting for Democrats could send you to hell.

Referring to the "intrinsically evil" practices of abortion, euthanasia, embryonic-stem-cell research, human cloning, and same-sex marriage, Ricken wrote, "Some candidates and one party have even chosen some of these as their party's or their personal political platform. To vote for someone in favor of these positions means that you could be morally 'complicit' with these choices which are intrinsically evil. This could put your own soul in jeopardy."[8]

What makes religious leaders think they can meddle in partisan races like this? Part of it is just hubris. American bishops tend to an unruly flock. Polls show that large numbers of Catholics disagree with the hierarchy over issues such as birth control, divorce, gay rights, abortion, and even core church doctrines. But the bishops keep trying, desperately believing that if they just crack down even more, people will fall in line. Good luck with that.

Groups within the religious Right are also to blame. These groups spread an alarming amount of misinformation. Every year, the ADF distributes reams of misleading materials to members of the clergy. The group claims, for example, that tax exemption for churches is a constitutional right. In fact, the Constitution says nothing about tax exemption for houses of worship or any other group.

Tax exemption is a matter of custom, not constitutional mandate. It's hard to say exactly when the practice got started, but some scholars have noted that during the Roman Empire, Pagan temples were exempt from taxation. The Romans were consummate bureaucrats who had refined tax collection to an art form. They had to in order to pay for the state apparatus that protected and managed their sprawling empire. In all likelihood, tax exemption was transferred from Pagan temples to Christian churches during the Christianization of the empire in the fourth century. The practice was established in Western culture and carried to America during the period of European settlement.

The Supreme Court stated in a 1970 case, *Walz v. Tax Commission,* that property tax exemptions for houses of worship don't violate the First Amendment provision barring "establishment" of religion. The court did not say that such exemptions must be granted or that they are mandated by the Constitution—it merely said that to grant them is not a violation of the separation of church and state.[9]

Nor has any court ever accepted the argument that partisan political intervention in campaigns by nonprofit entities is a protected form of free speech or freedom of religion. The ADF's claims that this is so are made up out of whole cloth. The group is clearly hoping that the IRS will sanction a church for stepping over the line and that it can take this case into the courts. Why the ADF wants this—aside from the fact that it would use such a case to raise money—is unclear, considering what happened to the ACLJ in the Church at Pierce Creek case.

In the case of the ADF and its allies, such as the ACLJ, the Liberty Counsel, the Family Research Council, and other religious

Right groups, there is an additional benefit to church politicking: it allows for the creation of a church-based political machine that can, in many cases, propel the Far Right's favored candidates into office.

During the 1990s, I spent a lot of time following the activities of the Christian Coalition, a religious Right political group founded by TV preacher Pat Robertson. The Christian Coalition was clearly trying to build a Far Right political unit that would rival some of the powerful political machines of the past. Robertson even talked openly about this, expressing his admiration for Tammany Hall and the Byrd Machine in Virginia.

But there was a problem: it was slow going. In a pre-Internet age, even dedicated volunteers were having a hard time finding people to form the machine and making sure they voted. The effort was very labor intensive. I remember attending Christian Coalition meetings where staff members or chapter leaders would talk about canvassing neighborhoods, making phone calls, and collecting information about each voter on index cards or in a computer file. The idea was to locate and target the "right" kind of voter (and I mean *right* in more ways than one) and then make certain that person voted on Election Day.

As I said, this took a lot of work. Some people just weren't up for it. In some parts of the country, the coalition was very powerful; in other regions, it barely had a presence.

Eventually, this model was discarded for a better idea: the creation of "voter guides," thinly veiled campaign literature that made it clear you should vote for the most conservative Republican in a given race. These guides would then be distributed in right-leaning evangelical and fundamentalist churches (as well as the few Catholic churches that might agree to take them on).

As I said, these guides were in no way fair. They were deliberately skewed to make certain candidates look like sinners and others saints. The coalition used several tricks to pull this off. One was to highlight certain issues over others; another was to distort how issues were described. Simply lying about a candidate's views was always an option as well.

One of the coalition's sleaziest tactics was to list, say, ten issues and, for a Democrat seeking office, put "No Response" for eight of them. The other two would have a response. The clear intent was to lead the reader of the guide to assume that the candidate had responded to the two issues and ignored the rest. A person looking at the guide might conclude, "The candidate is dodging these eight issues. He must have something to hide!" In fact, the candidate had decided not to cooperate with the coalition and had ignored all ten. The two responses were simply made up or allegedly taken from a public vote or statement.

Getting these guides into churches was the key to the strategy. From the right's perspective, it made perfect sense. Instead of canvassing a neighborhood and attempting to smoke out the political views of residents (only to find out, in many cases, that they were of the wrong type), the coalition identified large, fundamentalist churches, where it was safe to assume that most people were already into Far Right politics, and mobilized them.

For various reasons, the Christian Coalition went into steep decline during the George W. Bush presidency. But other groups picked up the church-based electioneering strategy and ran with it.

Obviously this strategy could not work if the biased voter guides were determined to be campaign material that favors one candidate over another. Houses of worship may not legally distribute such material.

This is what "Pulpit Freedom Sunday" and similar efforts by the religious Right are about. It's not about "freedom" or "religious liberty." It is yet another strategy designed to give the religious Right political power so its leaders can tell you what to do. It is a giant scheme designed to politicize the Far Right churches whose congregations consist mainly of fundamentalist busybodies who sit at home every night, bemoaning the fact that gay people continue to exist and that public schools dare to teach evolution. This is all about forging a political machine, not furthering religious freedom.

Groups like the ADF give a little lip service to the idea that all churches should be able to jump into partisan politics. And there certainly are some left-leaning congregations that have stepped over the line. But the left has nothing like the organized and systematic campaign to violate federal law by endorsing or opposing candidates that the religious Right champions.

The left doesn't want this. Neither do most Americans, for that matter. Numerous polls have shown that strong majorities oppose pulpit-based politicking. Many factors may motivate this, but the message is coming through loud and clear: most Americans simply don't look to their pastors for advice on how to behave in the voting booth.

There is another factor at play as well. While right-wing, fundamentalist megachurches may not have much political diversity, most other congregations do. The men and women sitting in the pews are aware that a pastor's overt politicking on behalf of a certain candidate will likely divide the congregation. Pastors know this too.

Most Americans look at their house of worship as a place for spiritual solace. They go there to get closer to God and to engage in acts of worship with fellow believers. They aren't necessarily interested in being lectured on whom they should support in the upcoming gubernatorial election. They can figure that out for themselves.

In a nation that is increasingly split by the red-states–blue-states divide, Americans see houses of worship as areas of refuge. They are places to put aside raucous political debates and focus on what unites us, not what divides us.

Of course, many fundamentalist churches are an exception. Far Right fundamentalists and the ultraorthodox of many stripes have a tendency to politicize everything. In their confusion, they have even dragged their houses of worship, which they claim to treasure, into the dirty and worldly work of partisan politics. They would use their churches as vehicles to influence the political system in the hope that political leaders will then impose a rigid morality—a morality that, ironically, their pastors have been unable to persuade people to accept voluntarily through their preaching.

It's a strange situation, and, at times, I can conclude only that some fundamentalist churches long ago lost faith in Jesus. Sure, they still talk about him, but their main emphasis seems to be the mayor, the governor, or the president. They continually believe that a "moral" America will come from politics. It's not something their savior preached, but they have adopted it. At religious Right gatherings (I've attended plenty over the years), one doesn't hear much talk about Jesus. The emphasis seems to be on the next presidential election (and no matter which one it is, it's always the most important one the country will ever face, every time) or who will be Speaker of the House of Representatives.

This leads us to the next question: What exactly is the role of religion in politics? We've already looked at the legal aspects. We know what the IRS says houses of worship *can* do in the political sphere. But what *should* they do? It's a much more challenging question.

Religious Right leaders often assert that those of us who favor a secular constitution and a secular government want to totally divorce religion from politics. We are accused of believing that religious groups should have no voice, that they should focus strictly on things like prayer and worship.

There may be some people who feel that way. We live in a big country, and opinions on this matter run the gamut. That shouldn't surprise anyone.

But I think the situation is much more nuanced than the religious Right would have us believe. Most Americans are fine with religious groups speaking out on the issues of the day. It's a pretty common thing, after all, and most people have encountered it and are comfortable with the concept of religious groups having a public voice.

That does not mean they agree with what religious groups are saying on political issues. And here is where things get dicey.

Any group that enters the political fray should expect pushback. People often talk about *controversial issues*, but that term is something of a redundancy. If an issue is in the public mind, it is by its very nature controversial. People will have strong opinions about it.

Some religious groups have equated strong opposition to their political views with an attempt to deny them their right to speak. To be fair to religious groups, this is a fairly common assumption in America's political give-and-take. People unfairly assume that a spirited counterargument must also involve a desire to cut off someone's access to the microphone.

Not necessarily. Most Americans are quite capable of listening to a position that does not conform to their own—and formulating a counterargument.

What offends many secularists, I think, is that some religious leaders (and I'm careful here to say just some) seem to believe that their views and political opinions, because they are wrapped in theological dress, are somehow above criticism.

We get this a lot from fundamentalist-Christian groups and sometimes the Catholic hierarchy. Their view seems to be that certain issues aren't even worth debating because the church, by the very nature of its religiosity, has access to some type of higher truth that transcends differences of opinion among people.

When challenged on this, these religious leaders often point to universal moral truths. Religions have condemned murder for eons, they assert. That may be true (although in the Middle Ages, clerics put their stamp of approval on plenty of murderers), but it overlooks the fact that universal moral truths are precisely that— universal. Secular people hew to them as well. The attempt to iden- tify these principles as the sole property of religion is offensive because it implies that those outside the religious system do not hold them and, thus, aren't really moral or ethical people.

In reality, many secularists argue that their morality is equally worthy of respect, and perhaps even more so since it does not hinge on fears of punishment or desires for a reward.

This debate was summed up nicely by the nineteenth-century

Portuguese novelist José Maria Eça de Queirós in his novel *The Maias*. In one scene, an old man who is raising his grandson discusses the boy's education with a priest:

> "Well, now, and what would you teach him, Abbe, if I handed the boy over to you?" asks the old man. "That one should not steal money from people's pockets; nor lie; nor ill-treat inferiors—because all this is against God's Commandments and leads one to hell, eh? Isn't that it?"
>
> "There's more to it—" begins the priest, but the old man cuts him off and says, "I know that. But you would teach him not to do any of these things because they're sinful and offend God. However, he already knows he should not do them because they are unworthy of a gentleman and a decent man."
>
> "But, senhor—" the priest attempts to interrupt.
>
> Concludes the old man, "Listen, Abbe. There's all the difference here. I want the boy to be virtuous for the love of virtue, and honorable for the love of honor; not fear of hell's kitchen, nor lured by the bait of heaven."[10]

Those who advocate for separation of church and state are often frustrated by the attitude—common among right-wing religious groups—that only certain religious believers have access to morality and, consequently, that their theology must guide society, otherwise there will be chaos.

This is a common strain of thought among the religious Right. I've heard it espoused numerous times at right-wing meetings over the years. The problem with it is that it places certain issues outside the realm of debate because the implication is that the Bible, the pope, the Book of Mormon, the teachings of a guru or some other religious authority have ended the need for debate. Most of the time, these issues that conservative religious groups have settled by quoting the Bible or "natural law" or whatever are the ones Americans are most eager to debate—legal abortion, gay rights, the role of women in society, increasing religious pluralism, and so on.

This is a good time to point out the glaring flaw in this argument: what is being appealed to by the religious Right isn't so much a holy book or a pronouncement from a band of bishops as it is some person's *interpretation* of that document.

I hear religious Right leaders and their followers throw around the word *biblical* a lot. They demand a "biblical" society or call for a return to "biblical" values. It drives me crazy. They aren't pushing for a country based on the Bible; they are pushing for a society based on their interpretation of the Bible. Those are two very different things.

Let's put aside the question of whether it's actually possible to build a biblical society. (Have you read the long list of laws in the Book of Leviticus lately?) What I have seen over the years is classic cherry-picking. Religious Right leaders hoist the Bible—a long and sprawling work fashioned together piecemeal over many centuries and written during a prescientific age—and demand that it take precedence over the Constitution.

To the religious Right, the Bible is a civics text. It's also a law book, a history book, a science text, a geography book, and so on—no matter how many errors and contradictions it has been shown to have. Because the tome is so long, right-wingers can find support for virtually any position in the Bible.

They have been playing this game for a long time. When the Confederate States of America sought to buttress slavery, they pointed to passages in the Bible. When segregationists opposed racial equality, they cited Bible verses. When women demanded rights, opponents in the conservative churches pulled passages from the Bible to oppose them. When LGBTQ Americans sought to end discrimination, again the Bible was used to block them.

In every instance, someone else came along, pointed to the very same Bible, and argued that it didn't say those things. The passage had been misinterpreted. Or it was written for a different time and a different place. Or it was no longer applicable.

Both camps are Christian. Both camps are sincere. Yet both cite the same book. That's one reason we don't base our laws on books some people deem holy—no one can agree on what they say.

But let's say, for the sake of argument, that the Bible was open to only one interpretation on these matters. It would still be irrelevant. Why? It's the Bible. It's a religious book designed to provide theological guidance. It's not the Constitution, nor was it ever intended to be.

Religious Right activists often assert that without the Bible as a guide, we don't have a standard to determine morals. Some assert that the default then becomes moral relativism.

As it so happens, the standard these people want is always their own. But let's give these folks the benefit of the doubt for a moment. Actually, a standard is not a bad thing. And we do have one. It's outlined in our Constitution. Our standard can never be a religious one, however. Why not? As I've pointed out several times so far, we don't agree on religion. People generally tend to think that what they believe about religion is correct, yet interpretations vary widely. To adopt one "standard" over another makes the government a theological referee. Other countries have tried that. It's a nightmare.

Far from being treated with kid gloves in the political arena, religious groups should be subjected to the same level of scrutiny that any other interest group receives. When lobbyists for a giant corporation descend on Capitol Hill and fan out to make the rounds of the offices of the House and Senate, we don't just assume they have our best interest at heart. We know better. They're after something for themselves, and we may like it or we may not, but we sure want to know about it.

Why would we treat religious lobbyists differently? Simply because they are religious? No. We have an obligation to look at what goals religious lobbyists are trying to achieve whenever they approach legislators and to judge those goals the same way we would the goals of any secular lobbying group. In the case of the religious Right, it's often just another attempt to gain power over us. Heightened scrutiny is called for.

We have the right—indeed, the *obligation*—to ask certain questions of these religious groups. For example, are you trying to expand rights or take them away?

Religious Right groups often compare their political activity to the efforts by houses of worship to oppose racial segregation during the civil-rights era. Both instances involved cases of churches getting involved in a political issue, but that's where the similarity ends.

What the religious Right is doing in this case is attempting to cloak whatever political campaign it has under way in the noble garment of the civil-rights movement. Hardcore racists aside, most Americans look back on that era and appreciate the contributions of all the activists, whether they were religious or secular, in helping to build a fairer, more-just society.

The civil-rights movement was an attempt to advance freedom, not retard it. Activists of that era saw that a segment of our population was being subjected to discriminatory laws and policies, and they sought to change that. It was expansion of rights, not a reduction of rights.

Compare that to some of the contemporary campaigns led by religious Right groups. In several states, the religious Right led efforts to add amendments to state constitutions barring marriage for same-sex couples. They sought to restrict rights.

In other states, religious Right groups led drives for new restrictions on abortion. Again, they were reducing rights. Religious Right efforts to force their narrow version of religion into public schools are no different. They are about the reduction of rights, not their expansion. When creationists work to remove instruction about Darwinian evolution from public schools, the only right they are promoting is the right to be ignorant of modern science. The attack on the freedom to learn, no matter what form it takes, is always a collapse of rights as well.

Conservative religious groups have pursued a very clever strategy in the public arena. They have deliberately conflated criticism of their political agenda with criticism of their faith. As I said, this strategy is deliberate. The idea is to put religious groups beyond the reach of legitimate criticism by portraying attacks on their political goals as a type of crude attack on religion itself. In a religious nation like the United States, this confusion only serves to benefit religious organizations.

We must cut through this fog machine and make one thing clear: a person is quite capable of believing that individual Catholics have the right to worship as they please and take part in whatever rituals are meaningful for them while still opposing having his or her healthcare governed by Catholic dogma. A person is quite capable of supporting a fundamentalist Christian's right to go to church and pray as he or she sees fit while still opposing any and all efforts to replace public-school science instruction with implausible tales mined from biblical literalism.

We have the right—again, some might say the duty—to demand that right-wing religious groups justify their policy objectives in some way other than simply pointing to the Bible or papal pronouncements.

When these groups are speaking to their own kind at, say, a national gathering of the religious Right, speakers don't even try to offer secular arguments for their goals. They openly talk about their interpretation of the Bible and act as if Jesus personally came back to put his stamp of approval on everything they are trying to do.

In courts of law (and, to some extent, in the court of public opinion), these groups are required to at least take a stab at a secular argument. Watching them try to fashion one can be amusing.

In controversies over school prayer, for example, religious Right groups often argue that prayer isn't really about communicating with God. A religious Right leader who would never tell that to his followers at a private meeting will, with a straight face, insert this argument into a legal brief. Public prayer, we're told, merely provides for a moment of reflection or is meant to solemnize an occasion.

Attempts by the religious Right and the Catholic bishops to find nonreligious reasons why same-sex marriage should not be permitted have been even more creative. "We don't much like it" isn't really a legal argument, so these groups were left to grasp for something more. They were not very successful.

In legal briefs filed before the Supreme Court in a pair of LGBTQ-rights cases in 2013, the religious Right and the bishops placed a lot of emphasis on procreation. This was nothing new. They had been making that argument for years. But they really leaned on the argument before the high court, not having much else, and ended up sounding like purveyors of a fertility cult.

Procreation is a great thing for those who want it, but not all do. Some couples are childless by choice. Others are simply too old to produce offspring. Still others are infertile due to medical conditions. If procreation is the ultimate end of marriage, all of these couples could be denied the right to marry, a fact not lost on several Supreme Court justices during oral arguments.

The Catholic bishops at least attempted to drum up another nonreligious argument: they asserted, apparently with straight faces, that the government should not recognize same-sex marriage because it would result in discrimination against the Catholic Church! The argument went something like this: if marriage equality becomes the law of the land, Catholic churches will be forced to accommodate it in various ways, and they fear it will jeopardize their access to government grants and contracts. They complained of being marginalized.[11]

As I noted elsewhere in this book, such marginalization, if it occurs, will be a cultural phenomenon. By the end of the civil-rights era, most of the population was no longer interested in finding ways to keep racists happy. If the same thing is happening again with gay rights, so be it. The bishops are essentially arguing that the government must deny an entire class of people their rights because otherwise, the Catholic Church's increasingly antiquated views will be called out for what they are: grossly out of step with the times. It's remarkable.

Sad as it was, we have to at least give the bishops some credit for trying. In other venues, they are accustomed to releasing a smoke-screen of theological gobbledygook about "natural law," inherent values, or some other verbiage that sounds impressive at first but boils down to, "We're right because our religion says we are; you have to listen to us." It sounds nice in the pulpit, I suppose, but it's not much of a legal argument.

The sad thing is, none of these groups ever learn from their mistakes, and the tide of history just keeps rolling over them. The Catholic hierarchy fought liberalization of divorce laws for many years. But most Americans decided they didn't want church dogma to govern their relationships, and laws changed.

As I discuss in the chapter on culture, Catholic bishops and their evangelical Protestant brethren for many years had the power to control what people saw and read. State and local government maintained censorship boards that bowed to religious Right demands for "purity." But people grew tired of giving religious zealots veto power over the books and magazines they read and the films they saw, and laws changed.

Religious conservatives reacted with alarm when women began to press for rights. They fought against the vote for women, and decades later mobilized when the modern women's rights movement was born. A woman's natural role, they argued, was as a wife and mother. But women (and plenty of men) came to realize that rigid gender roles no longer made sense, and laws changed.

When LGBTQ Americans argued for their rights—at first, simple things, like the right to speak and march and even be visible—right-wing religious bodies hit the panic button. But attitudes began to change, and now laws are changing too.

In every case, religious conservatives could do nothing but point to the Bible or papal decrees as movements for justice and equality bypassed them. Other, more-progressive religious groups greeted the changes with glee and even led the drive in some cases. The right wing remains entrenched in place, stuck like a wooden fence post in cement that slowly rots as the years go by.

And every time, these same religious conservatives warn darkly that if the rest of the nation fails to heed them, disaster will befall us. Yet the disaster never comes. Indeed, we turn out to be a better and stronger nation because we have extended rights to another marginalized group and welcomed them as full and equal partners in the American experiment.

I'm sure this is troubling to the religious Right. Consider it from their perspective: For hundreds of years, they held an incredible amount of power over the lives of people. Even as recently as the 1950s, American Catholics tended to defer to the bishops on matters such as family planning and the education of children.

But the clerics' grip started to slip. For many reasons, Americans began to shake off clerical shackles. They didn't turn against religion—this is not western Europe. What Americans did was find ways to reconcile their beliefs about their private lives with the teachings of their chosen faith community. When this absolutely wasn't possible, they found another faith community.

Imagine the effect this had on conservative clergy. How dare people make up their minds about their sex lives? How dare they engage in family planning? How dare they explore issues of spirituality outside the box of conventional religion?

I've said several times in this book that when we're trying to understand the motives of the religious Right, it's helpful to take a step back and look a little deeper. What's really going on here? We must do the same with the issue of politics.

The short answer is that religious conservatives called the shots for a long time for everyone, and they would like to have that power back. This isn't about religious freedom; it's about control. Religious groups have freedom—the freedom to speak, to act, to spread their views. But they no longer have the power to control others. It was taken away from them by the very people they sought to control. That smarts.

Of course, they still have control in other nations. The Catholic Church, for example, continues to meddle in the internal political affairs of the Philippines as well as several African and South

American nations. Fundamentalist Islam holds sway in many nations.

But in the West or in nations with a strong Western tradition—including much of Europe, Scandinavia, North America, Australia, and others—ultraconservative religious groups have much less power than they had just fifty years ago. In most of these nations, they won't be getting it back because demographic trends have led to secularization as a political and cultural reality. (The short answer: a lot of people quit going to church.) But in the United States, which retains a strong church-going base and a great interest in things spiritual, the reactionary religious brigades see that they still have a shot.

So they seek to limit access to legal abortion, make it harder to get birth control, besiege public schools, labor to have their sacred symbols erected at the seat of government, push to roll back the rights of LGBTQ folks, and so on. In some states, they receive a very welcome reception, but less so in others.

The culture wars drag on, even though many of us are weary of them. But above the din, we should remember one thing: this is not about religious freedom or any religious group's right to speak. They have been speaking for a long, long time. Fewer people may be listening, but that's no one's fault but their own. Maybe if what religious conservatives had to say weren't so toxic, larger numbers of us would listen in more often.

Religious Right groups say they just want to be heard. They are heard. In a country were right-wing Christian radio and TV dot the land and Far Right ministries reach out to people over the Internet and social media, these groups cannot plausibly argue that they have no voice.

They have a voice, all right. They are certainly heard. Being heard isn't really what they want. What they want is to be followed.

They have had plenty of opportunities to make their case. In the case of the Catholic bishops, they've been at this game for two thousand years and are well represented in America. Alongside them, fundamentalist-Protestant ministers thunder from thousands of pulpits every weekend. Their doors are open for all who choose to enter them.

The problem, as the bishops and their fundamentalist allies see it, is that too many Americans don't want to buy what they're selling. Americans can be stubborn, and I mean that in a positive way. It's one of our most charming attributes. While most respect religion, it doesn't mean they are interested in following the dictates of someone else's faith by force.

Religious conservatives have had plenty of opportunities to make their case. Has it ever occurred to them that maybe they haven't made it very well? What they have failed to achieve through moral persuasion they now seek to implement at the point of the state's sword.

No, thanks. Americans know better. They know something innate that eludes the sensibilities of the religious Right: in this country, where the right of conscience is precious, all religious groups have the right to be heard—but none have the right to be obeyed.

6

CULTURE

It has been a long time since American law recognized the concept of blasphemy, but there are those in the religious Right today who would love to revive the concept. Their attacks on the arts—visual media, literature, film, music, and stage plays—are a long-running feature of American life.

In examining the Far Right attack on culture—both high culture and its lower-brow cousin popular culture—we see a familiar pattern: Ultraconservative religious groups once called the shots and enjoyed censorship power over many art forms. In the modern era, that power was stripped from them through a combination of court rulings and public demands that religious censorship be rescinded. It was, and religious conservatives are mad.

It's an old story. Much of the world's great art explores religious themes. These treasures fill museums around the world. Many were produced during an era where, in Europe, the purpose of art was considered to be the exaltation of the Christian faith.

But times change. Religious conservatives seem to have a hard time grasping that.

Even back in the day, not everyone was willing to play along. Around 1800, Spanish painter Francisco José de Goya completed what is considered one of his greatest works: *The Naked Maja* depicts a young woman, completely nude, reclining on a couch.

Although considered a masterpiece today, the painting scandalized some religious leaders of the time. In Spain, where the Catholic hierarchy held sway, Goya was summoned before the Inquisition in 1815—yes, it still existed then—and grilled about the painting, which church leaders labeled "obscene." Interestingly, they demanded to know who had commissioned the work. History does not record what Goya told them, but whatever it was, it saved the painting. Today *The Naked Maja* is on display at the Museo del Prado in Madrid.

Flash forward to 2010. Conservatives triumphed in the midterm elections and were feeling empowered. What was one of the first things they did? They attacked a work of art.

In December of 2010, before US representative John Boehner (R-Ohio) had even been officially sworn in as Speaker of the House, he and some fellow conservatives blasted the National Portrait Gallery in Washington, DC, over its display of a brief video that had been deemed "sacrilegious" by the Far Right Catholic League for Religious and Civil Rights and other right-wing groups.

To hear Boehner and other members of Congress tell it, it would seem that the video in question was being run on JumboTrons in the museum under flashing neon lights with a sign reading, "This way to the perverted video!" In fact, the video in question was part of a much larger exhibit titled "Hide/Seek: Difference and Desire in American Portraiture," which explored through art questions of gender identity in American history.

You can probably see what the real problem was—that pesky gender identity! The exhibit contained works by several artists, including Georgia O'Keeffe, David Hockney, Jasper Johns, and Andy Warhol. The controversial video was made by the late David Wojnarowicz, a performance artist who worked in several media. Titled *Fire in My Belly*, it was about four minutes long; an eleven-second segment shows ants crawling on a crucifix.

Why did Wojnarowicz include this image? It's possible he wanted to attack the Catholic Church (although that seems a rather subtle way to do it), or he might have just thought ants were interesting creatures. Some art critics believed that Wojnarowicz, who died of AIDS in 1992, was making a statement about the suffering of those who have the disease, but Wendy Olsoff, a gallery owner in

New York City who represents Wojnarowicz's estate, said the artist viewed ants as a microcosm of human society and often showed them crawling on lots of different objects in his works.

"It was not about Christ," Olsoff told the *Washington Post*. "It was just about institutionalized religion."[1]

Nevertheless, the Smithsonian Institution, which has jurisdiction over the National Portrait Gallery, yanked the entire video after Boehner and US representative Eric Cantor (R-Virginia) attacked the work.

"American families have a right to expect better from recipients of taxpayer funds in a tough economy," Kevin Smith, a spokesman for Boehner, told the *Washington Post*. "While the amount of money involved may be small, it's symbolic of the arrogance Washington routinely applies to thousands of spending decisions involving Americans' hard-earned money."[2]

Cantor went beyond that; he demanded the entire exhibit be shut down. He called it an "outrageous use of taxpayer money and an obvious attempt to offend Christians during the Christmas season."[3] This led another leading congressional foghorn, US representative Jack Kingston (R-Georgia), to up the ante. He insisted that Congress launch an official investigation into the matter.

Note that Boehner, Cantor, and Kingston didn't hesitate to label the brief video image offensive and an attack on Christianity. This is a common practice among those who engage in religious censorship. They never hesitate to assume the role of art critics. They're akin to the guy in the old cliché: they don't really know what art is, but they know what they don't like.

Unless Boehner, Cantor, and Kingston managed to channel Wojnarowicz from beyond the grave or to stumble upon an explanation of the video he left behind, they have no way of knowing what he meant by it. It's possible he included the image because he thought it was interesting.

Smelling blood in the water, William Donohue, president of the Catholic League, insisted that the exhibit was an example of "hate speech." In a press statement, Donohue lauded the removal of the video but asserted that the Smithsonian Institution should have never allowed it in the first place.

Again, Donohue is no art critic and had no idea what the artist meant by the piece. All he knew was that he didn't like it—so no one else should either, and it certainly should not be displayed in a public museum. Thus, Donohue's artistic sensibilities, such as they were, would have become the standard for everyone.

The flap at the National Portrait Gallery was hardly unique. In a celebrated case from 1999, Rudy Giuliani, then mayor of New York, attacked the Brooklyn Museum of Art for displaying an image of the Virgin Mary by artist Chris Ofili (himself a Roman Catholic) that included a piece of resin-coated elephant dung.

Once again, the Catholic League went on the attack, this time joined by then archbishop John O'Connor. Giuliani was seriously bothered by the art and tried to cut off city funding for the museum and even evict it from its quarters. Legal action ensued, and a federal court blocked the Giuliani overture. (All of this was going on while Giuliani was involved in a high-profile split from his wife, who had left him after finding out that he had been seeing another woman. Giuliani's tendency to complain about exhibits like this led *Saturday Night Live* to poke fun at him during its mock newscast. The anchor intoned that Giuliani had angrily declared he doesn't want to see perverted art when he visits a museum with his mistress.[4])

My employer, Americans United for Separation of Church and State, was dismayed by the flap at the National Portrait Gallery. Americans United believed that the kerfuffle over the Smithsonian Institution was a sign of things to come and perhaps would become yet another front in the religious Right's ongoing efforts to stoke the flames of the culture wars. Publicly funded museums looked like low-hanging fruit.

Americans United noted that the National Endowment for the Arts and the National Endowment for the Humanities have been in the religious Right's crosshairs for years.

In December of 2010, Americans United joined the National Coalition against Censorship and twelve other organizations to protest the action at the National Portrait Gallery. The groups noted that conservative religious groups have no right to demand that public art conform to their narrow version of theology.

"The Catholic League may insist that religious symbols are its property and others (especially homosexuals) cannot use them; however, a national museum is barred by First Amendment principles, as well as by its mission to serve all Americans, from enforcing those views on the rest of us," asserted the joint statement. "The Smithsonian, of which the National Portrait Gallery is part, is a public trust serving the interests of all Americans. It betrays its mission the moment it ejects a work whose viewpoint some dislike."[5]

Flaps like this seem tailor-made for the religious Right and its allies in the Far Right media machine. You can almost see the headlines: "Your Tax Dollars Paid for Elephant Dung!" These attacks overlook the fact that controversial art accounts for very little of what appears in publicly funded museums.

Anyone who has been to any of the Smithsonian museums in the nation's capital realizes that they are national treasures. Most of what appears in those museums is conventional art, often created by the great masters. Some of the museums do display modern pieces that defy simple explanation. I'll admit that I've looked at some of these works from time to time and shook my head, thinking, "I don't get it."

But as I kept looking, I realized what I was doing: trying to get it. Maybe I did and maybe I didn't. I might even go home and talk to my wife or to a friend about what makes for real art. Who knows? Maybe that is what the artist wanted me to do all along. I look at it this way: any time I emerge from an art exhibit, a movie theater, or even the pages of a book asking questions and thinking about what I've just seen or read, I'm ahead of the game. I've been given something. I regard that mental exercise as a gift.

One of my problems with religious censors is that they don't seem to want us to get that gift. They don't want us to see a challenging piece of art or read a "blasphemous" book because it might make us think. They'd rather we not think, because when we think, we might start to challenge some of the assumptions conservative religious leaders would prefer to spoon-feed us.

Think of it this way: Most of us have, at some point in our lives, made some significant change in our opinions. Maybe you dropped a political position that you long held and came to embrace the opposite view. Perhaps you discarded a religious view you were brought up in and joined another denomination or left religion entirely.

Most people, when they talk about these types of changes, will say something like, "Well, I started having doubts—and then I read this book . . ." Over the years, I've talked with hundreds of ex-fundamentalist Christians, ex-Catholics, ex-Mormons, ex-you-name-it, and they all tell that story. Sometimes people will acknowledge that a friend or a family member challenged their beliefs as well, but sooner or later, a book enters the picture.

Most of us can site at least one book that we consider life changing. I know that for me, I was never quite the same after reading *The Great Gatsby* in the tenth grade. It wasn't that the book's message alone was so powerful. It was that, until then, I had been mainly reading genre fiction, and the concept of a literature of ideas was alien to me. The idea that a work of fiction could do more than tell a story—that it could explain the human condition—was new to me, and exciting.

Some people would rather we not have encounters like this. They fret about the places this type of inward reflection may take us.

Sadly, the religious censor applies the same rough screen to all works, the classic and the cornball. Someone like Donohue, who tends to see anti-Catholicism lurking just about everywhere and seems to have no sense of humor, can't quite grasp that books and films come in degrees. Yes, sometimes people do want to be intellectually challenged. Other times, they just want to be entertained.

In 2009, Donohue went ballistic over the release of the movie

Angels and Demons. Based on the popular novel by Dan Brown, the film centers on various intrigues at the Vatican and focuses on a plot that I'm told is rather fantastic. Donohue demanded that the movie include a disclaimer saying it was fictional, but even church officials disagreed, seeing the movie as harmless summer fluff.

As a film critic, Donohue leaves something to be desired. In 2004, he lapsed into an anti-Semitic rant while defending Mel Gibson's movie *The Passion of the Christ.* Appearing on the Fox News Channel, Donohue thundered, "Hollywood is controlled by secular Jews who hate Christianity in general and Catholicism in particular. It's not a secret, OK? And I'm not afraid to say it. That's why they hate this movie."[6]

If only he had been afraid to say it! The nation would have been spared another anti-Semitic conspiracy theory. As he rambled on, looking grim and dour, Donohue was undoubtedly unaware that he looked exactly like the last guy on the planet you would choose to safeguard your entertainment options. Left up to him, you'd probably be limited to books by Fulton Sheen, movies from the 1950s featuring Bing Crosby as a friendly priest, and perhaps reruns of *The Flying Nun*—perhaps.

We've been down this road before. The United States lived through a period where Donohue and his pals called the shots when it came to arts and entertainment. It was an awfully long time, but we managed to shake off their grip. There's no going back. We're not going to let religious prudes tell us what we can read, see, or hear again.

That does not mean they won't try. As I've noted many times already, this crew really misses being able to lord it over us. They'll do anything to get that power back.

The Catholic bishops and their factotums are old hands at this. "Decency" crusades used to be their stock-in-trade. The church hierarchy in Europe enjoyed a stranglehold over publishing for hundreds of years. It took them longer to get a foothold in America, but when they did, they came on strong.

In 1933, a Catholic bishop in Cincinnati formed a group called the Catholic Legion of Decency to combat alleged immorality in movies. The organization soon drew support from some conservative Protestants, and the following year, it changed its name to the National Legion of Decency. Its membership, however, remained heavily Catholic.

The legion asked its members to sign a pledge condemning "indecent and immoral motion pictures" and vowing to "remain away from them."[7] The idea was that Hollywood would respond with more-wholesome entertainment.

So far, so good. The pledges were voluntary, although the legion later began pressuring film studios to abide by a "voluntary" code governing film content. Like most censors, the legion had a tendency to go overboard. It condemned the zany 1959 Marilyn Monroe comedy *Some Like It Hot* for cross-dressing.

The plot of this film deals with two male musicians who get into trouble with gangsters. To hide out, they dress as women and join an all-female band. It has troubled fundamentalist zealots for a long time. Alan Sears of the Alliance Defending Freedom, a religious Right legal group, has also attacked it. He likely disapproves of *Tootsie* as well, and let's not mention *Mrs. Doubtfire*.

The legion managed to apply enough pressure that some directors shifted operations overseas to avoid trouble. But the legion's victories were temporary. By the 1960s and '70s, the country was seeing the rise of a grittier, more action-oriented cinema that dared to address social issues. By the 1970s, films were becoming more risqué, and an ostensibly voluntary "production code" that many religious groups had supported was abandoned by the big studios. The legion became defunct and was subsumed into the hierarchy of the Catholic Church, which, through its Catholic News Service, continues to review films today and labels many as "morally offensive."

Such rating systems, offered to people who are free to follow or reject them, are a far cry from past practices, when some religious figures labored to prevent anyone from seeing certain films or reading some books.

The decency crusade wasn't limited to films. In 1955, researcher Paul Blanshard published *The Right to Read*, a book chronicling various literary censorship efforts, many led by religious organizations. Blanshard notes that these groups enjoyed great success for many years.[8]

During the great era of "vice suppression" in the 1920s and '30s, cities like Boston and New York were famous for banning books. New England's Watch and Ward Society (originally known as the New England Society for the Suppression of Vice) was so powerful that all its leaders had to do was apply pressure to booksellers to make certain volumes unavailable. In Boston libraries, books deemed objectionable were kept in locked rooms. (Thus the origin of the phrase "Banned in Boston.")

It's true that much of this material was of questionable merit— but much was not. That's one of the problems with censors; they cast a very wide net. Many of the books censored are now considered classics. Books targeted by the moral crusaders included Sinclair Lewis's *Elmer Gantry*, Theodore Dreiser's *An American Tragedy*, Upton Sinclair's *Oil!*, and Ernest Hemingway's *The Sun Also Rises*.

Writers, editors, and publishers were often rankled by the vice crusaders and began to fight back. In 1926, journalist H. L. Mencken traveled to Boston after learning that copies of the magazine he edited, *American Mercury*, had been removed from newsstands because they contained a hard-hitting story about a prostitute.

Mencken provoked a court challenge by openly selling copies of the magazine and sparking his own arrest. The case became a cause célèbre and put an uncomfortable spotlight on Boston's censorship practices. Mencken was acquitted.

Echoes of literary censorship are still heard today, mainly in the context of public schools. A recent example occurred in 2011, when the school board in Republic, Missouri, voted to ban two books— Kurt Vonnegut's *Slaughterhouse-Five* and Sarah Ockler's *Twenty Boy Summer*—after a local resident (who, by the way, didn't actually live in the district) complained that the books teach ideas contrary to the Bible. A third book, Laurie Halse Anderson's *Speak*, was also targeted but retained.

A huge backlash erupted to the board's vote after the story went viral. The Kurt Vonnegut Memorial Library in Indianapolis announced that a donor had provided funds to make free copies of the novel available to 150 students in Republic. Under pressure, the Republic board voted to return the books to the school library but with a catch—*Slaughterhouse-Five* and *Twenty Boy Summer* were placed in a special area (as if they were asbestos or something), and high-school students could check them out only if a parent or guardian did it for them.

The work of the censors increased as film became a more popular medium, and religious groups began turning their attention to the silver screen. For many years, filmmakers submitted to the Motion Picture Production Code, popularly known as the Hays Code, which prohibited, among other things, nudity, profanity, "perversion," miscegenation, and "ridicule of the clergy."

Religious leaders had input into the code and helped draft it. It held sway for many years but began to break down in the 1950s. A case soon reached the Supreme Court that tested the limits of religious censors, which hastened the demise of the Hays Code.

In 1950, an Italian filmmaker named Roberto Rossellini released a short film called *The Miracle*, the tale of a peasant woman who is convinced that the stranger who impregnated her is really Saint Joseph.

Outraged Catholic leaders in New York City insisted that the "sacrilegious" film be banned, and government officials were only too happy to comply. Church pressure was so intense that New York officials even revoked the license of the movie's distributor, Joseph Burstyn. But Burstyn fought back in the courts. His legal effort reached the US Supreme Court, which ruled unanimously in his favor in 1952.

"Since the term 'sacrilegious' is the sole standard under attack here, it is not necessary for us to decide, for example, whether a state may censor motion pictures under a clearly drawn statute designed and applied to prevent the showing of obscene films," wrote Justice Tom C. Clark for the court. "That is a very different question from the one now before us. We hold only that under the First and Fourteenth Amendments a state may not ban a film on the basis of a censor's conclusion that it is 'sacrilegious.'"[9]

Burstyn v. Wilson was an important ruling because it derailed states' ability to censor films on grounds of blasphemy and sacrilege. The decision also made it clear that film, like the printed word, falls under the scope of the First Amendment's guarantee of free speech. (As strange as this may seem, this was not clear in 1950. In handing down *Burstyn*, the high court overturned a 1915 decision, *Mutual Film Corporation v. Industrial Commission of Ohio*, that had declared that movies were not entitled to First Amendment protection because they were purely a commercial enterprise.)[10]

Although official censorship boards began to lose power after the *Burstyn* ruling, the Hays Code was not fully abandoned until the late 1960s. At that point, it was replaced with the Motion Picture Association of America ratings system that is familiar to moviegoers today.

Code or no code, some church officials continued to target movies they disliked. A major brouhaha erupted over director Martin Scorsese's 1988 film *The Last Temptation of Christ*, a film that brought out picketers in some cities. Several local governments—including Dallas, Birmingham, and a few parishes in Louisiana—passed symbolic resolutions condemning the movie (which, many lawmakers admitted, they had not seen).

Some went beyond symbolic resolutions. In one community, Escambia County, Florida, the county commissioners voted four-to-one to ban the film and actually sent a sheriff's deputy to the one local theater planning to show it to seize the print.

It's hard to believe that the cloak-and-dagger-esque drama that subsequently unfolded took place in twentieth-century America, but it did. Author Thomas R. Lindlof, in his 2008 book *Hollywood under Siege*, writes that the owner of the theater got wind of law enforcement's pending arrival, handed the print to a business associate, and sent him to the next county. The man checked in to a hotel with the censored film and hunkered down while lawyers for the theater worked in court to have the ban invalidated. It wasn't long before a federal judge struck down the ban.[11]

Religious censors often come off as killjoys, and for good reason—they are. H. L. Mencken's observation that the definition of a Puritan is someone who is plagued by the "haunting fear that someone, somewhere, may be happy" rings true here.[12]

Nowhere has this been borne out more than in the field of popular music. The pattern here is so familiar, it's depressing to contemplate that it keeps being recycled. Popular music—and by this I mean genres aimed largely at young people—has been blamed for just about every social ill over the years. Back in the days when vinyl was king, there were occasionally mass burnings of records sponsored by conservative religious groups.

Anything this side of Mel Tormé was a problem. Elvis Presley's gyrating hips were too much for some, and even the squeaky-clean (early years) Beatles came under fire. Rock and roll, it seems, was just too dangerous for kids.

Virtually every band that enjoyed popularity in the 1960s and '70s was attacked for something—often for promoting drug use or just generally for seeking to lead young people down the wrong road. The struggle against rock music was often portrayed in apocalyptic terms. In the late 1970s, when punk started to take off and the Sex Pistols gained a following in England, some people seemed to believe the survival of Western civilization was at stake. (Listen to "God Save the Queen" today—it sounds positively staid.)

Did some bands go over the edge with deliberately provocative lyrics and outlandish garb? Of course. How else were they supposed to excite rebellion in bedrooms all over the suburbs?

A little teen rebellion through music is not such a bad thing.

I'm sometimes surprised to hear baby boomers blasting the musical choices of their own kids. Don't they remember what was like to be sixteen? Shocking mom and dad with your edgy bands is part of the script. What surprises me is that some boomers, who probably dropped plenty of acid while grooving to the Jefferson Airplane back in the day, don't get this. (I turned eighteen about the time that punk bands were first becoming popular in America. I once joked with my teenage daughter that she shouldn't even try to offend me with her music. Nothing could outdo some of the punk bands I listened to.)

By the 1980s, with the resurgence of heavy metal bands, some ministers tied to the religious Right were blaming rock and roll for promoting Satanism. I have in my files an amusing document titled "History of Rock and Roll: Major Influence Chart," which appeared in a conservative Christian newspaper late in 1987.[13] An accompanying article warns darkly, "Experiments show that plants shrivel up and turn away from rock music while they actually thrive to the other." Elsewhere, this same insightful publication points out, "There is some evidence that much of the nervous problem in America was actually started by the Beatles!"[14]

The chart warns that the 1980s saw the rise of "Theatrical Satan Rock," and "lyrics even promote suicide." It observes, "MTV brings Satan's music into homes through rock videos." (Yes, kids, there was a time when MTV actually played music videos!)

My favorite part of the chart is the list of performers. "Satan Rock" is exemplified by some usual suspects: Kiss, Iron Maiden, AC/DC, Black Sabbath, and Alice Cooper. But also listed are the Eagles and Cyndi Lauper.

The Eagles? This '70s-era soft-rock band was hugely popular but rarely associated with the Prince of Darkness. My mother was a fan. She never suspected a thing. As for Lauper, her bubbly pop was catchy and would have driven some to distraction before hell.

Eventually things got to the point where a conspiracy theory entered the picture. Bands and record companies, we were told in the 1980s, were in cahoots to plant subliminal messages on records, which you could plainly hear when you played them backward. This was the infamous "backward masking."

I should back up for younger readers: before music was "CD-ized" and digitized, vinyl records were a popular medium. Many turntables did have the ability to operate in reverse, though I've never been clear why. Some genius got the idea to begin spinning rock records backward and started hearing all sorts of interesting things. Usually, they were exhortations to take drugs, worship Satan, and have sex—preferably all in the same evening.

As a college student, I was assigned by the school newspaper to attend a speech by a Christian evangelist who promised to offer a lecture exposing this nefarious plot. The event consisted mainly of him carping about the continued existence of AC/DC (for which I had some sympathy, being more of a New Wave fan then) and playing muddy recordings of the alleged subliminal commands. It all sounded like so much gibberish to me, and I never could understand the mechanism through which these secret messages were to reach your brain. The preacher capped things off with an altar call. All things considered, it wasn't one of my better evenings.

Backward masking never made a whole lot of sense to me. Wouldn't it be more effective simply to write songs overtly extoling the joys of dope and cheap sex? Some bands surely did that. Why backward mask anything when forward and unmasked guaranteed that the message got through?

The decline of the turntable and vinyl as a medium ended the mini-furor over backward masking. (As far as I know, you can't spin a CD backward or put your MP3 player in reverse.) Plus, as I noted, some bands were simply choosing to put their controversial messages right out there. Did some of them assail organized religion? You bet. Few targets were left unscathed then, and, during the '80s—an era of TV-preacher scandals and the growth of big-haired evangelists who promoted the "prosperity Gospel"—the fringes of religion were easy targets for critics.

Undoubtedly, some bands went out of their way to provoke the neo-Puritan brigade. The song "Dear God" by the English band XTC is an unapologetic paean to atheism. It was immediately banned in Britain, which helped with sales, I'm sure. Perhaps that was the point.

But even pop songs, like poetry and literature, can be open to interpretation and shrouded by shades of nuance. Were the Rolling Stones literally advocating sympathy for the devil in 1968? Some religious groups seemed to think so, and there were rumors at the time that the Stones were into Satanism. A more likely scenario might be that they were just making a statement about the corrosive effects of violence, perhaps asserting there's a little of evil in all of us.

Fundamentalists often have a difficult time grasping nuances like this. Theirs is a very black-and-white world, and, since they interpret the Bible literally, they have a tendency to treat other works the same way.

They also have a tendency to look for simple solutions to complex problems. The spate of violence and school shootings in the 1990s and 2000s led some conservatives to blame soft targets like black metal music and violent video games. To some people, there's a type of comfort in assigning the blame to one source rather than dealing with the complex issues that lie beneath such tragedies.

The fact is, pretty much every form of music since 1900 has been accused of leading youth astray—jazz in the 1920s, rock and roll in the 1950s, acid rock in the 1970s, heavy metal and punk in the 1980s, rap and hip hop since then. If popular music were the destructive force so many religious conservatives believe it is, society would have collapsed a long time ago.

I would be remiss if I left this topic without discussing one other important front in the religious Right's assault on culture: how Americans celebrate religious holidays, specifically Christmas.

A few years ago, Americans started hearing a lot about the "war on Christmas." I'm not sure which religious Right organization came up with this term, but it was given currency by the American Family

Association (AFA) in Tupelo, Mississippi. For the AFA, the war on Christmas was truly the gift that kept on giving. They used it to boost their media profile, raise money, and attack their political opponents. The AFA and its allies became what I call the "Christmas Police"—a repressive force that was bound and determined to ensure that everyone celebrated the holiday in the appropriate religious manner.

Was there really a war on Christmas? Only in the fervid imaginations of the Far Right. You might have noticed that Christmas is a pretty popular holiday in the United States; even many non-Christians celebrate it. So who would launch such a war, and to what end?

It turns out there were two trends under way, operating at the same time, that occasionally overlapped and that were affecting the celebration of Christmas in America. The religious Right disliked both of these trends and attempted to derail them by insisting that a war on Christmas had been declared.

There was no such war. What is happening is that the way the holiday is celebrated is undergoing a form of cultural evolution, and this troubles the religious Right and its Christmas Police.

The first trend is secularization. Here I refer to secularization as a cultural, not legal, phenomenon. In short, the religious aspects of Christmas aren't as prominent these days as religious conservatives would like them to be. They assert that this is due to some sort of coordinated war against the holiday and a deliberate effort, by some nefarious force, to deemphasize its religious aspects.

Is that what's really going on? Not at all. As I said, Christmas is a popular holiday. Most people have no interest in waging war against it. The reality is that Christmas has been a victim of its own success. It has become so popular that most people in America now celebrate it, including many non-Christians. But Christmas has always had secular *and* religious components. Because not everyone shares the religious components, it's not surprising that the secular aspects have become more prominent. The secular aspects of the holiday (elves, Santa Claus, reindeer, decorated trees, snowmen, candy canes, etc.) are seen as symbols that most people who celebrate the holiday will include. The religious symbols (mainly depictions of the nativity) are not. Some people celebrate Christmas as a secular holiday and don't include them.

Merchants and the owners of businesses want to make money. One way they do this is by pitching their products to as many people as possible. Messages that might alienate or, worse yet, anger some potential customers are avoided. Thus, many businesses use decorations, symbols, and themes that are heavy on the secular symbols of Christmas and don't include religious depictions. (It's also possible that some merchants might feel that using religious symbols in their stores borders on sacrilege. Do you really want to see a nativity scene in a giant discount store next to a stack of cheap, plastic snow shovels?)

Some religious conservatives and the Christmas Police have even been offended because clerks in stores might say "Happy Holidays" instead of "Merry Christmas." I feel sorry for anyone whose holiday is ruined because he or she failed to get the proper religious greeting from a cashier. But more to the point, some people say "Happy Holidays" because there is more than one holiday celebrated at the end of the year.

Every year in Tupelo, national headquarters of the Christmas Police, employees of the AFA scrutinize a variety of store advertising circulars and websites and count up the number of times the word "Christmas" appears. The AFA then prepares a "Naughty and Nice" list of retailers—those who use the word "Christmas" are nice, and those who do not are naughty.

I am not making this up. The AFA produces this list every year. And every year I feel sorry for the legions of the temporary employees they probably bring on to help with this chore. I once read that in Victorian England, some truly desperate people went about the streets collecting dog waste, which was used in the process of leather tanning. Being a member of the AFA's Christmas Police doesn't sound like a much better job.

For added fun, some companies seem to enjoy messing with the AFA. My wife and I receive catalogs from the Vermont Country Store, a large and popular mail-order firm. I've noticed that in December, some of their catalogs will be labeled "Christmas" and some "Holiday." Is the firm naughty or nice? Or maybe both at the same time?

The formation of the "Naughty and Nice" list is just the first step. The results are then reported to the Fox News Channel, which is the religious Right's stalwart ally in promoting the fictitious yuletide war. Religious Right groups and the Fox News Channel usually start whining about the war on Christmas before Halloween. I really do believe that Fox hires people (again, probably seasonal employees) to scour Google News every day for words like *Christmas, nativity scene, holiday tree*, and the like. They then pounce on any controversy and call the American Civil Liberties Union or Americans United and demand to speak to a top general in the war on Christmas.

Terms mean a lot to Fox and the religious Right. For a few years running, they threw a fit because in Rhode Island, Governor Lincoln Chafee called the large evergreen displayed at the statehouse a "holiday tree."

Even Roman Catholic bishop Thomas Tobin of Providence got in on the act. Tobin called Chafee's terminology "most disheartening and divisive" and said the governor's action is "an affront to the faith of many citizens."

Really? Chafee could have called the tree a "seasonal evergreen display" or even "that holiday thingy" and people would have known what it was. Do terms really matter that much? And is it divisive to use a term that is actually more inclusive? Here's a news flash: Christmas is going to come either way. In fact, the Rhode Island incident, many commentators said, had more to do with politics than Christmas. Tobin and his conservative coreligionists didn't like Chafee because he was seen as being too liberal on social issues; they looked for any reason to attack him.

That's one of the more discouraging features of the war-on-Christmas claims. One often gets the sense that the whole thing is just a plot stirred up by the religious Right and its pals at the Fox News Channel to assault liberals. "Look at those crazy liberals! They're so out of step with the mainstream that they're even attacking Christmas! What will they do next! Vote Republican and save Christmas!"

The sad thing is, this cynical manipulation of Christmas is being engineered by right-wingers—the same people who claim to value the holiday so much. To me, that's the real war on Christmas. People who truly value the holiday would not use it as just another prop to score cheap political points.

The secularization of Christmas is the first issue that has disturbed the religious Right. The second trend is the effort to uphold separation of church and state by blocking government-sponsored religious displays.

The Supreme Court has issued a string of rulings dealing with religious displays on public property. Some of these displays are permissible, and some are not. The question often turns on who put up the display, who is paying for it, and whether the space it occupies has historically been used for free-speech activities.

I don't intend to expound on these rulings here in detail. My point is that there is a legitimate controversy over the issue of government erecting religious displays. Many people—and not just nonbelievers—feel that the government has no right to put up religious symbols. When the government does that, the message being sent is that the state has a favored religion, and here it is. We put its symbols right here in front of city hall or the statehouse for all to see.

Over the years, there has been a good bit of litigation over this question. Cases often arise in December, when some local and state governments put up holiday decorations. If these decorations include religious symbols and signs, some people might conclude that church-state separation is being violated and file lawsuits.

To the right wing, this is another manifestation of the war on Christmas. But it's not. It's an attempt to uphold the separation of church and state. People are quite capable of supporting Christmas and even celebrating it while advocating for church-state separation. Some people involved in this litigation are themselves very religious and argue that the government should not usurp sacred religious symbols for its own ends. Others are offended to see the baby Jesus lying in his manger next to Frosty the Snowman.

The people who challenged government-sponsored school prayer in public schools in the late 1950s and early '60s were not engaging in a "war on prayer"; they were simply trying to uphold their rights. Those who defend the separation of church and state by challenging government-erected religious displays during the holiday season are doing the same.

Indeed, many of the church-state cases we see in December are also designed to remind America that things have changed since 1950—a concept religious conservative have great trouble with. Government imposition of Christian language and symbols isn't welcome (nor does it make sense) in a nation of so many faiths.

Alongside the legal disputes over religious holiday displays, there are often battles over how public schools deal with Christmas. Attempts by religious Right groups to use Christmas to impose their narrow version of faith onto young children are perhaps among the most obnoxious things they do. The script usually goes like this: Some type of clearly inappropriate religious pageant is planned for a public school. Someone gets wind of it and complains. The event is either cancelled or blocked by a court. Many in the community go ballistic and scream that Christmas is under attack or that the holiday has been ruined.

If the holiday has been ruined, it was ruined by the school officials who planned an unconstitutional activity, not the people who stood up for their constitutional rights. It never seems to occur to anyone in charge that perhaps the pageant belonged in a church all along. (I guarantee you, it would have occurred to them if the pageant had been a Druidic celebration of the Twelfth Night holiday.) Our public schools must serve children of many faiths and philosophies. Christmas events that emphasize the religious aspects of Christianity and promote Christian worship aren't appropriate for that diverse audience. Again, this is about maintaining a healthy separation of church and state, not knocking Christmas.

Humans seem to need a December holiday. Many religions have them, and they often feature the same elements: lights, greenery, and promises that the world will emerge from the winter darkness and life-sustaining crops will grow again.

For example, classical Pagans of ancient Rome celebrated a holiday called Saturnalia, many features of which were incorporated into Christmas. Today, many modern-day Pagans mark the solstice. The December holidays serve many functions, not the least of which is giving people a chance to celebrate during what can be a dark, cold, and gloomy time of the year.

How people mark this transition from darkness to light, from cold to warmth, from death to rebirth would seem to be up to them. The need to do it is there. How it is done is up to you—at least, that's what most of us would conclude.

Not the religious Right and the Christmas Police. And here lies the crux of the matter. All the carping about the war on Christmas is yet another attempt by religious conservatives to run the show. To them, there is one way to celebrate Christmas—their way. You can either do that or get out.

I call this type of intolerance "religious correctness." It must be opposed at every turn. This is America. We have real religious freedom here, not the fake version favored by fundamentalist zealots. This means you can spend the entire day of December 25 in church if you like. Or you can stay at home with friends and family and exchange gifts, never once mentioning the name of Jesus Christ. You can celebrate some other holiday. You can erect a Festivus pole and call for feats of strength. You can also ignore the holiday entirely and do nothing.

This infuriates members of the religious Right. How dare you celebrate the holiday in a manner that does not meet with their approval!
How dare you secularize December 25! How dare you add in elements
from other faiths! How dare you make the holiday your own!

We dare because we can. We have the right. Just as we have the
right to change our religious beliefs, convert to a new faith, or drop
religion completely. How that infuriates the religious Right! To that
intolerant movement, you have no right to equate your false beliefs
with its true ones. And make no mistake, the constant attempts by
adherents of the religious Right to make über-religious Christmas
the gold standard and weld it with the government are designed to
send a not-at-all subtle message: We're in charge here. We're the
bosses. The government likes us better than you. Our holiday is
first class; your thing is second class.

There is no war on Christmas. There is instead a band of well-
organized, well-funded, and determined fundamentalist zealots
who believe they have the right to tell you what to do—even when
it comes to celebrating a December holiday. Let's be as clear as a
bright, winter day: they have no such right.

Furthermore, nothing you, I, or anyone else does (or doesn't
do) in late December affects these folks or reduces their Christmas
celebration *one iota*. I've yet to meet an atheist who spent Christmas
Eve or Christmas Day trying to stop Christians from going to
church. I'm not aware of any organized effort to prevent any church
anywhere from erecting a nativity scene on its front lawn. I know
of no plan to stop the sale of religious Christmas hymns on CDs or
through iTunes. There is no scheme to block the release of holiday
DVDs with religious themes.

The simple fact is, Christmas can be as religious as you want it
to be. Most churches are happy to throw open their doors in late
December and welcome everyone. There's no shortage of concerts
featuring religious music, depictions of living nativity scenes, special
programs and service projects at houses of worship, and so on.

The problem, as the religious Right sees it, is that some people have chosen a Christmas that isn't religious enough. Those who spout religious correctness, those who yearn to control others, would love nothing better than to rule over Christmas like a Dark Ages emperor and issue fiats about how we are to celebrate.

Those of us who support real religious freedom will resist the Christmas Police at every turn. We regard such resistance as a duty because we know what the principle of religious liberty really means: the right to decide for ourselves what, if anything, Christmas—and, by extension, any religious event—means to us. And we know what the phony war on Christmas really is. It's a desperate last gasp from a faction of ultraconservative religious zealots who can't come to grips with the simple fact that they no longer own American culture.

To them I say, "Welcome to the twenty-first century—and Happy Holidays."

PERSECUTION

Certain words should not be tossed around lightly. *Persecution* is one of those words.

Religious Right leaders and their followers often claim that they are being persecuted in the United States. They should watch their words carefully. Their claims are offensive; they don't know the first thing about persecution.

One doesn't have to look far to find examples of real religious persecution in the world. In some countries, people can be imprisoned, beaten, or even killed because of what they believe. Certain religious groups are illegal and denied the right to meet. This is real persecution. By contrast, being offended because a clerk in a discount store said "Happy Holidays" instead of "Merry Christmas" pales. Only the most confused mind would equate the two.

We have worked hard in the United States to find the right balance concerning religious-freedom matters. Despite what the religious Right would have Americans believe, this is not an issue that our culture and legal systems take lightly. Claims of a violation of religious freedom are usually taken very seriously. An entire body of law has evolved in the courts to protect this right. The right of conscience is, appropriately, considered precious and inviolable to Americans.

Far from being persecuted, houses of worship and the religious denominations that sponsor them enjoy great liberty in America. Their activities are subjected to very little government regulation. They are often exempt from laws that other groups must follow.

The government bends over backward to avoid interfering in the internal matters of religious groups and does so only in the most extreme cases.

What the religious Right labels "persecution" is something else entirely: it is the natural pushback that occurs when any one sectarian group goes too far in trying to control the lives of others. Americans are more than happy to allow religious organizations to tend to their own matters and make their own decisions about internal governance. When those religious groups overstep their bounds and demand that people who don't even subscribe to their beliefs follow their rigid theology, that is another matter entirely.

Before I delve into this a little more, it would be helpful to step back and take a look at the state of religious liberty in the United States today. Far from being persecuted, I would assert that religion's position is one of extreme privilege.

Consider the following points:

- Religious groups enjoy complete tax exemption, a very powerful and sought-after benefit.
- Unlike secular nonprofit groups, houses of worship are not required to apply for tax-exempt status. They receive it by mere dint of their existence. Houses of worship are assumed to be tax exempt as soon as they form. This exemption is rarely examined again and is revoked only in cases of extreme fraud (such as someone claiming that the entity he or she has formed is a church when it's really a for-profit business).
- Houses of worship are free from the mandatory reporting obligations that are imposed on secular nonprofit groups. For example, secular groups that are tax-exempt must fill out a detailed financial form and submit it to the Internal Revenue Service (IRS) every year. This document, called a Form 990, must be made available for public inspection. Houses of worship and ministries are not required to fill out and submit these forms.

- Religious entities are not required to report their wealth to any government agency. The question often comes up about how much money houses of worship raise every year or what the value of the land they hold is. There is no way of knowing this because they are not required to tell anyone.
- The IRS has the power to audit individuals and secular groups at the merest suspicion of wrongdoing or financial irregularities. Houses of worship, by contrast, are very difficult for the IRS to audit. This is so because Congress passed a special law governing church audits that requires the IRS to show heightened scrutiny before initiating such procedures. In addition, church audits must be approved by highly placed IRS officials.
- Religious groups enjoy a loud and robust public voice. They own television and radio stations all over the country (all tax exempt, by the way). They own publishing arms, and they maintain various outreach sites on the Internet. The ability of religious groups to proselytize and spread their theology is limited only by the imaginations of their leaders.
- Across the country, religious groups own a network of hospitals, secondary schools, colleges, social-service agencies, and other entities that often enjoy a cozy relationship with the government. Many of these institutions are subsidized directly with tax funds—even though they may promote religion. In recent years, religious groups that sponsor charitable services have seen themselves open to a host of new taxpayer assistance through the so-called faith-based initiative.
- Religious groups are often exempt from laws that secular organizations must follow. A house of worship or a ministry can fire employees at will if those workers violate (or are merely suspected or accused of violating) some tenet of the faith. A religious school, for example, could fire a woman who becomes pregnant out of wedlock. A corporation or a secular nonprofit would not be able to do this.

- In many cases, religious groups are free from following even basic laws designed to promote health, safety, and general welfare. Houses of worship are routinely exempted from laws designed to improve access to facilities for those with disabilities, for example. In some states, daycare centers and other facilities sponsored by religious groups are wholly exempt from routine inspection laws.

- Many religious groups engage in extensive lobbying on Capitol Hill and in the state capitals. Under federal law, there is virtually no regulation of their lobbying activities. Federal law exempts from oversight "a church, its integrated auxiliary, or a convention or association of churches that is exempt from filing a Federal income tax return."[1] This means that, unlike other groups, religious organizations are not required to report the money they spend attempting to influence legislation or to register their lobbyists. In rare cases, some states have tried to impose minimal regulations, such as public financial-disclosure reports, on houses of worship. The religious groups often fight such laws and call them an infringement of their religious-liberty rights.

- Many legislators are quick to placate religious groups and the clergy. The results of their lobbying campaigns are often successful. In the 1990s, when some religious groups began to complain about experiencing difficulties with zoning issues and the ability to build houses of worship where they pleased, Congress was quick to pass a special law called the Religious Land Use and Institutionalized Persons Act. This law essentially trumps local zoning regulations with a federal fiat—even though, for many years, zoning had been considered a matter best handled by local officials.

- Religious groups are often treated with special deference in cases of suspected law breaking. Anyone who doubts this need not look beyond the experience of the Roman Catholic Church during the pedophilia scandal. A secular corporation

that engaged in such a massive cover-up and acts of deception would have found its top leaders behind bars. Yet in that
scandal, only a handful of relatively low-level clergy were
held accountable.

I have created this list not necessarily to criticize or call for
changing these policies (although some of them are overdue
for scrutiny) but to make the point that the leaders of religious
organizations have very little reason to complain. Their position
is an exalted one. They are well regarded by lawmakers, and their
institutions are not only tax supported in some cases but are also
beyond the reach of secular law. What they are experiencing is not
persecution; it is preferential status.

Why, then, is there so much complaining from the religious
Right? (And it does come primarily from religious conservatives.
Mainline and moderate clergy tend to understand their position of
privilege and appreciate it.) Why do we hear so many cries about
persecution?

Primarily we hear this because, despite their cushy position in
society, religious groups do not get everything they want. In the
case of ultraconservative religious groups, some of what they want
is unrealistic or would require a complete reordering of society
and perhaps a different constitution. In other words, our nation is
not the theocracy that many in the religious Right would prefer.
When they attempt to make our society more theocratic, plenty of
Americans resist. Our refusal to roll over and submit to them is, to
their mind, a form of persecution.

Evolving cultural trends have also led to a certain degree of
panic among religious conservatives. For years, they engaged in
gay bashing with abandon. They were confident that the public was
on their side, and for some years, the picture did indeed remain
murky when it came to questions of LGBTQ rights.

But then the pendulum began to swing. It's hard to say exactly
when this happened. Certainly by the late 1970s, attitudes toward

gays were changing. This shift was even reflected in the popular culture, with the introduction of sympathetic gay characters on television sitcoms and in films.

The trend continued throughout the 1980s and '90s. These early battles tended to focus over issues that sound jarring to today's ears. For example, in 1978, California voters faced Proposition 6, a measure that would have made it mandatory for public schools to fire gay teachers. The measure was defeated by nearly 60 percent, and even Ronald Reagan, then governor of the state, opposed it.

Mobilized by such campaigns, the LGBTQ community went on the offensive through legislative action and attempted to change public opinion, employing an organized campaign that had many facets. It urged gays to come out of the closet and make their sexuality known to friends, family, coworkers, neighbors, and so on. At the same time, it worked to dispel misperceptions about gays and debunk stereotypes.

Polls began to show a shift toward a position of tolerance. Religious Right groups were alarmed but continued to argue that public opinion was on their side. They even managed to win court victories. In 1986, the Supreme Court upheld a Georgia law that banned acts of consensual sodomy between adults. (In 2003, the ruling was overturned when a new case reached the high court.)

As years passed, public opinion on issues such as the ability of same-sex couples to adopt or gays to receive employment protection continued to change. In 2003, another milestone occurred when same-sex marriage became legal in Massachusetts in the wake of a ruling by the state's supreme judicial court.[2]

While the ruling may have cheered LGBTQ activists, it opened up another front in the culture wars. States became battlegrounds. Several states adopted constitutional amendments to bar same-sex marriage after campaigns led by the religious Right and, in the case of California, bankrolled by the Catholic Church and the Mormons.

Opponents of marriage equality looked to be on a roll. Then, in 2012, their momentum stalled. Three states—Maryland,

Maine, and Washington—voted for marriage equality. A fourth, Minnesota, voted down a state constitutional amendment barring same-sex marriage. Not long after that, public-opinion polls began to show, for the first time ever, majority support in favor of marriage equality. Among younger people, the question wasn't even close. One poll showed that 81 percent of younger Americans said they favored marriage equality.[3]

Statistics like this really put religious conservatives into a state of panic. It looked as if the work they had done to roll back same-sex marriage might be undone in the future.

As the national discussion shifted to marriage equality, something important was overlooked: how much ground the religious Right had lost over the issue of LGBTQ rights in general. Fifteen years ago, even most LGBTQ activists weren't pushing for same-sex marriage; many of them considered that a long-term goal. Suddenly the issue was thrust into the national spotlight, and indications were that public sentiment was shifting.

In the face of this, religious Right groups could do little but start to spin wild tales of persecution. They argued that they had been forced to accommodate LGBTQ Americans in certain ways, or that they soon would be.

Much of this was only so much carping, barely worthy of a response. Religious conservatives know full well that houses of worship in America can't be forced to give admission or provide services to anyone. Churches have an absolute right to determine their own membership and the qualifications for earning it. Some houses of worship have an open-door policy and more or less welcome everyone. Others are stricter.

Many churches, especially those affiliated with the more conservative end of the theological spectrum, apply certain moral standards or expect certain behaviors from their members. Those who run afoul can be counseled to correct their ways or summarily excommunicated. This is entirely a private matter. A person who is kicked out of a house of worship or denied membership has no legal recourse.

In light of this, it's difficult to determine where some religious conservatives got the notion that the government was prepared to make them do anything when it comes to gay rights. As I noted in chapter 3, the state has no power to compel houses of worship to perform same-sex marriages. The First Amendment guarantees against that.

Yet the rhetoric continues to escalate. In April of 2013, a right-wing radio talk-show host named Janet Mefferd made the inevitable Nazi comparison. Mefferd, who was angry after a public high school in Michigan cancelled a speech by antigay politician Rick Santorum, said she can see the "day when every Christian who supports real marriage might be made to wear a yellow patch on the sleeve, a 'badge of shame' to identify us as 'anti-gay haters.' Kind of like the Jews in Nazi Germany."[4]

I don't have to explain why talk like this is so off-base and offensive. It collapses under the weight of its own absurdity. Yet we hear more and more of it.

Why do some religious conservatives embrace such lurid rhetoric? They seem to be extremely troubled by the shifts of cultural opinion. They are aware that if current trends continue, their views on LGBTQ issues will become antiquated and, eventually, socially unacceptable. But note what I said: *socially* unacceptable, not legally. That distinction is crucial.

There was a time when some churches espoused racism and segregation. Few churches today would do this. Of course, nothing in the law would stop a church from espousing these views today, and who can say, there may be some on the fringes that still do. Churches dropped these views because of societal pressure, not government action.

The religious Right's beef, then, would seem to be with the direction of the culture. To be sure, the legislature and the legal system can sometimes push the culture along. When Massachusetts's supreme court ruled that marriage must be extended to same-sex couples, some residents of that state were undoubtedly upset. Some even lobbied for changing the state constitution to bar the practice. But that effort failed, and, in time, the waters calmed. No house of worship has been forced to admit gay members or perform services for them. By and large, most people seem to have moved on— except for a fundamentalist fringe.

It is not the job of the government to protect houses of worship from the backlash they may experience if their views on same-sex marriage (or some other issue) are perceived as antiquated and out of step with majority opinion. As long as that backlash takes peaceful forms and doesn't involve actual assaults on churches, the state has no obligation to intervene.

At times, it seems as if the religious Right's real problem is mere coexistence with LGBTQ Americans. This may sound harsh, but in listening to their rhetoric, it is sometimes difficult to draw any other conclusion.

In late March of 2013, Tony Perkins, president of the Family Research Council, appeared on a conservative radio program and warned that if the Supreme Court were to strike down state constitutional provisions barring same-sex marriage, a literal revolution might occur.

"If you get government out of whack with where the people are and it goes too far, you create revolution," Perkins said. "I think you could see a social and cultural revolution if the court goes too far on this."[5]

Perkins added that a ruling favoring same-sex marriage "could literally split this nation in two and create such political and cultural turmoil that I'm not sure we could recover from [it]."

It's difficult to conceive of the source of such rhetoric. If the past is any guide, the country actually does quite well with cultural change, despite problems along the way. Many people opposed the right of women to vote in 1920, but the alteration was made without violent revolution. The civil-rights era of the 1960s did, of course, spark violence, riots, and assassinations. But, in the end, the country held together and moved forward. We will survive the era of gay rights as well.

I think it's a safe bet that relatively few people are willing to take to the streets in armed conflict because same-sex couples are able to get married. Even in the heartland of America, in Iowa, where same-sex marriage was enforced by a judicial ruling in 2009, no civil war has arisen, and so far no one has seen fit to try to pull the state from the union. Perkins speaks of turmoil so serious that the country could not recover. Yes, there has been some turmoil and sharp differences of opinion over same-sex marriage in the states where it is legal, but those jurisdictions have not been split apart, and succession movements, if they exist, aren't getting any traction. (As a matter of fact, the only state that regularly talks about pulling out of the union is Texas, which doesn't recognize same-sex marriage in any form.)

As of this writing, same-sex marriage was legal in California, Connecticut, Delaware, Hawaii, Illinois, Iowa, Maine, Maryland, Massachusetts, Minnesota, New Hampshire, New Jersey, New York, Rhode Island, Vermont, Washington State, and Washington, DC. I monitor church-state and religious-liberty issues very closely for a living. If any houses of worship or any member of the clergy had been persecuted in those states for refusing to serve LGBTQ residents or for speaking harshly of them, I would know about it. In fact, all of us would know about it. Such a story would gain national headlines. It hasn't happened.

The rights of religious groups in this area are secure. There is no persecution. We're much more likely to see fallout from private citizens who own businesses and who decide that, due to their religious beliefs, they will not deal with LGBTQ people.

There have already been some cases like these involving wedding photographers, caterers, florists, bakers, and others who refuse to provide services to same-sex couples. They say their religious beliefs preclude them from offering business services to these couples. Forcing them to do so, they argue, would be a form of persecution.

But is it really persecution? Remember, we're talking here about retail establishments, not houses of worship. Generally speaking, public-accommodation laws in the United States prohibit retail stores and establishments that offer services from discriminating on the basis of race, color, religion, or national origin. These protections are found in the Civil Rights Act of 1964 and were intended, in part, to address issues such as hotels and restaurants that refused to serve African Americans.

Sexual orientation is not included on the list of protected classes in federal law, but some states and cities do have laws that protect gays. No one would seriously argue today that forcing the owner of a business to end discriminatory policies is a form of persecution. It makes no difference if those policies are motivated by religious belief, it is still discrimination. Some Americans today are Islamophobic and don't want to deal with people who are Muslim or whom they perceive to be Muslim. Requiring that they do so, as the law mandates, is not persecution. It's an attempt to ensure a fair and just society.

A nondiscrimination policy doesn't prohibit anyone from worshipping as he or she pleases. It doesn't block that person from attending the house of worship of his or her choice, praying, reading religious books and so on. Such policies do require owners of businesses to serve the public. This is not too much to ask. Perhaps people who do not wish to serve all members of the public should not open shops, since the understanding is that retail establishments do, in fact, serve the public.

A second area where one often hears the cry of persecution involves public schools. As I've noted elsewhere in this book, public schools serve young people from a variety of religious and philosophical backgrounds. They are not the exclusive property of any one religious group. Yet fundamentalist Christians, looking at the schools and seeing all of those "unsaved" youngsters, can't help but salivate. They tend to view the schools as mission fields.

Public schools can never be that. Courts have been clear about this. That hasn't stopped the religious Right from trying. When they are curbed in their efforts to use the public schools for evangelism, they often cry persecution and assert that their religious freedom is being violated.

Religious freedom gives every student the right to pray in a public school in a private and nondisruptive way. Students may also read religious texts during their free time and engage in voluntary religious activities with their friends (again, in a nondisruptive way). Many secondary schools now have student-run religious clubs that meet during noninstructional time.

Why isn't this enough for the religious Right? It's because all of these activities are focused on individuals. They don't really allow for aggressive forms of proselytizing. And proselytizing is what the religious Right wants.

Public schools are a focal point for so many culture-war battles for a good reason: a lot of children attend those schools. No other institution provides such a large gathering of young people on a regular basis. Religious conservatives seek to use the nation's compulsory-school-attendance laws and network of public schools to spread their faith. A lot of people don't just resist this, they go to court to stop it.

Several recent cases have dealt with so-called student-led prayer at school events. Religious Right legal groups came up with this ruse some years back to get around earlier court rulings striking down compulsory prayer in public schools. Their thinking was that if teacher-led prayer in public schools was unconstitutional (and clearly, it was), the practice might survive if shifted to students. Federal courts have generally taken a dim view of the scheme, but this hasn't slowed down the religious Right.

Public-school graduation ceremonies are not like Speakers Corner in London, where anyone can get up and say anything. They are controlled events, often carefully timed and choreographed to send certain messages that school officials want to convey. Since these are public schools we're talking about, it's not surprising that one of these may be a message of inclusion: all students are welcome here. It's hard to send that message if a student hijacks the event and begins preaching.

At many schools, education officials ask to review the comments that the valedictorian or salutatorian plans to offer. This is acceptable because, again, a public-school graduation ceremony is not open-mic night at the local improv club. And it's not just inappropriate religious proselytizing that may be removed or curtailed. Any comments deemed not fitting for the ceremony or grossly off topic will likely be removed as well. This is not persecution because there is no constitutional right to take over a public school event and turn it into a quasi church service.

Likewise, we often hear claims of persecution when government refuses to help religious groups enforce their theology or spread sectarian messages. Earlier, I discussed the controversies that often arise over the presence of religious symbols on public land. On the occasions when courts order these symbols removed, claims are made of persecution.

Again, these claims are misguided. If the government invaded the sacred and private space of churches and attempted to tell clergy which symbols they could post on their own property, then that would indeed be persecution. It would not be tolerated. But that's not what's happening when aggressive religious groups are told they do not have the right to monopolize public space and link their symbols to government.

Americans United and the American Civil Liberties Union have been involved in several cases challenging the display of the Ten Commandments in public schools or at courthouses. These schools and courthouses are public, tax-supported institutions. They must represent and serve all people in the community, not just those who venerate the Ten Commandments as a holy document.

Defenders of the Ten Commandments often argue that the document is merely legalistic in nature. Anyone who takes the time to read it can see that this isn't true. Several of the commandments on the first tablet are religious in nature and have no counterpart in our secular laws. The clear purpose of displaying the Ten Commandments is to promote one religious view above others. This is made obvious by backers of these displays, who often talk about using the commandments to influence people's religious behavior.

It's not persecution to stop the government from endorsing one religious view over others. Our Constitution, the Supreme Court has noted several times, calls for neutrality on religious issues. It's not neutrality when the laws of a certain theological perspective are elevated to a position of prominence above all others. As I mentioned elsewhere in this book, the purpose of such displays is almost always to send a message: Certain believers are insiders with the government and enjoy its favor. All others are on the outside and are, at best, second-class citizens. If there's any persecution going on here, it's against the people deemed lesser citizens because they don't share the theology expressed on those tablets.

The government is not persecuting anyone or any religious group when it prevents them from trying to run the lives of others. Religious conservatives yearn to tell others what to do and to make their theology the supreme law of the land. The state can't help them with this; indeed, it has an obligation to protect the rights of others by ensuring that this does not happen.

The great irony here is that what the religious Right is trying to do—forge a government that bows to its repressive theology— would result in a great deal of persecution. We've had a taste of this already, and it's a bitter taste indeed. Across the country, legislators, prodded by religious Right groups, are trying to pass laws banning the imposition of Islamic law. (Newsflash for these guys: the First Amendment already bans the imposition of religious law.) Some of these measures are so sweeping or poorly written that they would ban purely religious practices that Muslims consider to be part of a personal law that is binding on believers of that faith.

In other cases, right-wing religious zealots have actually gone to court to try to block Muslims from building mosques on land that they own and that has been zoned for religious use. No legal argument is put forth in these cases, just bigotry. These same organizations often raise money and incite public opinion by trading in the crudest forms of Islamophobia. They stir up hate and turn American against American. And we're supposed to believe these very organizations are the ones being persecuted?

It's not persecution to tell someone to stop being a jerk or to demand that they respect the Constitution. It's not persecution to tell one group of believers that they must extend to other groups the same rights they themselves demand and even take for granted. It's not persecution to remind a band of religious extremists who are convinced that they and they alone possess religious truth that, while they have the right to believe such a thing, their zeal confers upon them no power to tell others what to do.

When the religious Right raises bogus claims of persecution, it belittles the sufferings of those believers who truly are persecuted. I would advise members of that movement to learn what real persecution is.

Go to Saudi Arabia, where it's illegal to even open a Christian church, and experience the fear of those Christian believers who dare to worship in private homes, aware that at any moment they may be imprisoned.

Visit North Korea, where all religions have been swept away and replaced with a bizarre form of worship of the state and its leader that purports to promote self-reliance but, in reality, merely serves as a vehicle for oppression.

Visit any region under the control of the Taliban, a movement so extreme that, in Afghanistan, they trashed that nation's cultural heritage by blowing up two sixth-century statutes of Buddha because they were declared false idols by religious leaders who are intolerant of any other faith but Islam.

There is real religious persecution in the world. Right-wing Christians in America aren't experiencing it. The fact that a same-sex couple may live on your block is not persecution; a huge department store choosing to display secular holiday symbols in December is not persecution. A court ruling enforcing the separation of church and state by removing sectarian symbols from the courthouse is not persecution.

Nor is spirited opposition to the political goals of religious groups persecution. Any group—religious or secular—that enters the political arena must be prepared for organized opposition to its agenda. Such opposition is certainly to be expected in the case of ultraconservative religious groups because their agenda is so controversial.

It's true that the rhetoric gets a little heated sometimes, and unfortunate things may be said. That's the rough-and-tumble of American politics. It's hardly persecution. In light of what I wrote earlier in this chapter about religious groups and their ability to lobby and their often-easy access to the offices of legislators, there would seem to be little ground for them to complain. Of course, many of them do complain—chiefly because, despite their unfettered ability to lobby in Washington, DC, and state capitals, they still don't get everything they want.

The right wing's persecution complex often goes hand in hand with another unfortunate trait: paranoia. In the 1990s, it was not uncommon to hear dark talk of "black helicopters" that supposedly harassed the right wing. Claims were made that Bill Clinton was planning to somehow remain in office after his second term ended, and so on. Admittedly, this stuff was more common on the very fringes of the right, but, like the various conspiracy theories centering around President Obama's birth certificate, these kooky claims would occasionally cross over to the large religious Right groups.

In 2010, I attended a meeting of the Family Research Council, the nation's largest religious Right organization and one that labors to portray itself as "mainstream." Among the speakers was a man named Dale Peterson, a garrulous cowboy from Alabama and a Republican Party activist. Employing borderline-racist rhetoric, Peterson took potshots at Obama's lineage, remarking, "I don't know what he is." After his speech, Peterson told a reporter that he does not believe Obama was born in the United States.[6]

The persecution complex and the paranoia give birth to a third phenomenon: an almost messianic belief that only Far Right religious conservatives can save the country from certain doom. In my years of attending religious Right gatherings, it's this talk that has struck me the most. I sometimes get the feeling that extreme religious conservatives, despite their frequent displays of hyper-patriotism and their tendency to venerate national symbols, such as the American flag, don't like the country much. Modern America is too secular, too gay friendly, too focused on sex, and so on. Every year these gatherings are predicated on the promise of a pending divine punishment that never seems to come (although some among the religious Right are sure that things like hurricanes, tornadoes, floods, and other bad storms are signs of the deity's displeasure). Backsliding, sin-obsessed America is due for a hiding very soon, speakers at these events love to say. The only thing that can save us is to allow fundamentalist religious zealots to make the rules for everyone.

Speakers at religious Right events love the concept of the false choice. One of their favorites is to insist that gay rights and religious freedom can't coexist. We must choose one or the other, so which will it be? During the 2010 meeting of the Family Research Council, I heard Bryan Fischer, a public-policy analyst at the American Family Association, explain this for the crowd.

"We must choose between the homosexual agenda and religious liberty, because we simply cannot have both," Fischer wailed. Again, it is the classic false choice. We can't have both? Who says? . . . Other than Fischer, that is.

To the extent that there is such a thing as a "homosexual agenda," and assuming it is represented in part by the legalization of same-sex marriage, then we already know that we can have both. Massachusetts has both. Iowa has both. New York has both. I am confident that, at some point not too far off from now, the entire nation will have both.

Of course, there are some things that can't peacefully coexist: democracy and theocracy, for example. Real religious liberty can't survive in the face of ongoing attacks by fundamentalists who are convinced that they have a God-given mandate to tell others what to do. One side will win, and the other will lose.

A religious Right legal group called the Alliance Defending Freedom (ADF) has a telling statement on its website. The group, despite its name, isn't really about defending freedom—except the freedom of a religious zealot to make moral decisions for you.

On its website, the ADF states that it "seeks to recover the robust Christendomic theology of the 3rd, 4th, and 5th centuries."[7] That's really the problem, isn't it? When leaders and members of the religious Right go looking for heroes of religious freedom, they don't turn to Roger Williams, Thomas Jefferson, James Madison, or even the Baptist preacher John Leland. They turn to Constantine the Great.

It's no surprise that many Americans would rather not live in a society governed by a fifth-century understanding of church and state. Many Americans believe that to even suggest it and hold it up as a good thing is alarming. Many Americans are going to do all they can to resist anyone or any movement attempting to impose that on them.

Standing up to and resisting this type of fundamentally anti-American interpretation of the relationship between religion and government is far from persecution. Many of us would consider it something quite different: good, old-fashioned patriotism.

CONCLUSION

RUN YOUR OWN LIFE, NOT MINE

I t's one thing to complain. It's quite another to propose some things that will make complaining less necessary.

We have a problem with the interpretation of religious freedom in America. Too many people believe that concept is a sword to use against others, not a shield with which to protect themselves. Too many people believe their faith makes them the logical candidate to tell others how to live. Too many people believe their religious beliefs give them the right to ignore laws they don't like. What's to be done?

Consider the question of access to contraceptives, which I've mentioned several times in this book. The issue can be summarized like this: The government wants people to have access to the medication they need—and, yes, it is medication. The Obama administration argues that access to birth control is an important medical goal for the country and an essential feature of women's rights. (I would argue human rights.) Religiously affiliated institutions assert that their rights are violated if they are compelled to contract with insurance firms that provide this service to employees who want it. Some owners of secular businesses say they shouldn't have to tolerate it in healthcare plans.

Who's right? Is compromise possible? The answers to these questions will do more than resolve a church-state dispute; they will determine what type of society we are or are striving to be.

Most of these disputes revolve around a handful of issues:

healthcare, LGBTQ rights, family law, privacy, and commerce. The key to resolution, I believe, rests in examining the types of entities that provide services to the public. Once we've recognized that these entities are not all the same and, thus, must abide by different sets of rules, a clearer picture emerges.

These entities can be categorized in one of four ways: government, private/religious, for-profit/secular, and quasi-public/church-affiliated. The confusion we face in this nation right now is that there is a deliberate attempt under way by some religious leaders to blur these categories—especially the last two.

This is being done for a reason. Religious groups want unfettered access to public funds but minimal regulations and oversight. They downplay religious freedom when seeking the former and invoke it when lobbying for the latter.

Is it any doubt this has spawned confusion?

When we look at the entities in question and see the ways in which they are different, it becomes easier to find a solution.

Government entities are perhaps the easiest to deal with and most susceptible to the application of bright-line rules. Put simply, the government's first duty is to treat all citizens equally; it must do so in a neutral manner that does not further religious interests.

In a state where same-sex marriage is legal, for example, the county clerk has no conscience right to refuse to issue a marriage license to any couple that legally meets the requirements for marriage. A clerk who refuses to do so can be terminated.

Likewise, an employee of a public hospital has no right to refuse to provide certain medications because they might offend her religious beliefs. In a government-run institution, personal theology must be kept out of all public policies and transactions. Government employees may have certain private religious rights—for example, the right to wear religious garb in certain cases or to be accommodated for time off to meet religious needs—but this right has never been interpreted as allowing infringements on the rights of others.

Private/religious entities are also open to broad rules and less susceptible to nuance. In such entities (churches, mosques, synagogues, temples, etc.), it's to be expected that decisions and policy will be governed by theological beliefs. Such institutions have no legal obligation to serve the general public. Indeed, they can refuse services and admission to any person for virtually any reason.

A priest at a Catholic church is under no legal obligation to marry a non-Catholic couple. Even Catholic couples can be subjected to theological dictates. For example, a couple that has been cohabitating can be required to establish separate households before the ceremony can be performed. Rules like this protect church autonomy and ensure that the religious Right's nightmare scenario of houses of worship being forced to perform same-sex marriages will never come to pass. The First Amendment principle of religious freedom prevents that.

In issues affecting healthcare, private religious entities have the right to impose whatever rules they want, no matter how out of step they may be with public opinion. Anyone who goes to work for a house of worship or a ministry, heads up a church project, or even serves as a sexton must understand and expect that all decisions concerning employment will be put through a religious filter. If a church believes women shouldn't work outside the home, it isn't required to hire any women. People who don't want to abide by these rules would do well to not seek or accept employment with wholly religious entities.

For-profit/secular entities, for the purposes of this discussion, are defined as businesses owned by a person who happens to be devoutly religious. The main thrust of most of these companies is secular. They may be factories, chain stores, restaurants, or manufacturing concerns. They are not in the religion business. As for-profit companies, they are subject to the same list of laws and regulations that govern any corporation. The owner's religiosity should not bestow upon him any special rights, especially in the way he deals with his employees (who may or may not share his faith). Thus, the government has the right to impose blanket policies on these companies to ensure that certain rights and benefits are accorded to employees, even if the owner believes these regulations offend his personal beliefs.

Quasi-public/church-affiliated entities present the biggest challenge and will be discussed in more depth. These organizations include church-run colleges, hospitals, and social-service agencies. They are sponsored by religious organizations but are often providing (directly or indirectly) a service on behalf of the government.

Generally speaking, quasi-public/church-affiliated entities can be categorized by three features.

They receive large amounts of support from the taxpayer. Religiously affiliated hospitals receive federal and state support through Medicare, Medicaid, and other taxpayer-funded programs. Students who attend colleges and universities run by religious groups are eligible for Pell Grants, low-interest student loans, and other forms of public financial aid. Sometimes, the institutions themselves receive direct government grants. Religious social-service agencies are often heavily dependent on taxpayer dollars. Catholic Charities, for example, receives more than half of its budget from government sources.

They hire people outside their faith tradition. Most church-run hospitals and colleges hire the best person for the job, regardless of the individual's religious or philosophical beliefs. Many religiously affiliated social-service agencies do as well, although some impose a religious test in hiring. (This has been a bone of contention over the faith-based initiative for years.)

They serve the general public. You don't have to be Catholic to go to Georgetown University or to get an operation at a Catholic hospital. In some cases, church-affiliated colleges will actively recruit outside the faith for students with special athletic or academic skills. Likewise, if you're having a medical emergency, a Baptist hospital will assist you even if you haven't been to church in years. In some cases, social-service agencies that accept tax funding are legally required to help everyone.

Certain religiously based accommodations have already been

made for these entities, especially hospitals. Catholic institutions, for example, won't provide birth control or sterilization, and the institutions are governed by a series of Catholic directives that cover issues such as end-of-life care. These accommodations are controversial in their own right, and many Americans believe no more should be granted.

These three factors set quasi-public/church-affiliated groups apart and make the imposition of bright-line rules all the more challenging. Yet some regulation is inevitable to ensure that public funds are spent in a way that accords with the public interest. Claims by some religious leaders that attempts to regulate them after the receipt of public funds are a violation of religious freedom are unrealistic and, I would submit, arrogant. Remember, these entities are not required to accept this money. If they don't want to meet accountability standards, then the answer is to not take public aid.

Tax funding is the key in dealing with these entities. None of them are required to accept public support, yet most eagerly seek it. When applying for (or sometimes actively lobbying for) tax assistance, these groups tend to play up their secular sides. They seem to acknowledge the value of secularism when tapping the public purse.

But it's a different story when regulations start to come. At that point, many quasi-public/church-affiliated groups begin stressing their faith-based side. "You can't impose that rule on us!" their leaders cry. "We're a religious group."

Such statements overlook the fact that the provision of tax money changes things in a very fundamental way. Thousands of secular corporations every year receive millions in tax funds to provide services to the federal government. (Defense contractors are a prominent example.) None of these contractors expects to be unregulated. Why do religious groups?

When public funds are involved, it is assumed that the entity in question is operating in the public interest and is answerable to the people. We've all heard stories about defense contractors spending $5,000 on a hammer. Stories like this shock the public conscience because they are examples of wasteful spending of public resources. They come to light because someone is tasked with investigating the groups that receive taxpayer support and ensuring that they are doing with it what they said they would. In these cases, the government has the right—many would argue the duty—to impose regulations to ensure that the public interest is protected.

Yet some religious groups are utterly blind to the public interest. They refuse to acknowledge that it even exists. Worse yet, they have deliberately sown confusion in the public mind over what types of entities qualify as purely religious and which are quasi-public.

The recent flap over birth control provides a good example of this principle in action. Many of the groups being affected are religiously affiliated yet quasi-public. They were offered a compromise, and most Americans see the compromise that has been struck as reasonable: houses of worship are exempt from the mandate that birth-control coverage be provided at no cost but religiously affiliated/quasi-public groups are not. For them, insurance providers will pick up the cost of birth control and inform employees of these entities that it is available. Religious leaders need do nothing that violates their right of conscience. Yet the compromise was still rejected by the Catholic bishops and their religious Right allies.

Worse yet, these groups played a religious-freedom card. They behaved as if the entities in question were the same as churches. They are not. Remember, churches are *wholly exempt* from the mandate. We are talking here about other types of places—hospitals, colleges, and social-service agencies.

Why the difference? A lot of it has to do with public support. Unlike churches, religiously affiliated hospitals, colleges, and social-service agencies actively solicit and accept huge amounts of tax aid. They also hire outside the faith and serve the public.

The hiring question is especially important and shows yet another distinction between purely religious and quasi-public institutions. People who go to work for a church are aware that they are doing religious work. Indeed, it may be what motivates them to take the job. Individuals who don't subscribe to the church's theology won't usually be hired.

Employees of church-affiliated hospitals or colleges often don't see it that way. A heart surgeon who is hired by a Catholic hospital is usually motivated by nonreligious factors. He or she may be only vaguely aware of the facility's religious ties—even though the owners and operators of religiously affiliated hospitals may talk about the provision of healthcare as a religious mission.

Many employees of such facilities see the institution's primary goal as the business of making sick people well, not making Protestants into Catholics or what have you. A largely secular service—healthcare—is being provided.

These factors open taxpayer-funded religiously affiliated entities up to reasonable forms of oversight to protect the public interest and individual rights. In an era where use of birth control has become near universal, it is simply unrealistic to allow a taxpayer-supported enterprise that operates in the public good to impose repressive theological dictates—rules that are so strict, even the vast majority of Catholics ignore them—on all Americans.

Equal treatment of all citizens is another compelling government goal that should influence this debate. Consider the issue of adoption, which has been controversial in certain states. In those states, government agencies directly oversee or facilitate adoptions. But they may also contract with religious agencies to provide this service and even give them tax funding to do it. In these cases, religious adoption agencies should be required to assess potential parents using neutral criteria. Denying adoption services to entire classes of people (gays, atheists, etc.) who fall short of a theological litmus test is rank discrimination. The government has the right—and, again, some would say the duty—to eradicate this type of discrimination.

The government also has the right to condition the receipt of tax aid on other relevant factors—for example, is the religious group seeking a government contract willing and able to do the job?

A recent flap over aid to victims of human trafficking provides a useful example. In this case, the US Conference of Catholic Bishops lost a federal contract because it had told its subcontractors that they could not provide birth control to victims of trafficking. The Obama administration believed that victims of trafficking—many of whom have been sexually assaulted or forced into prostitution— needed this service and awarded the contract to a group willing to provide contraceptives. Church officials claimed this was discrimination.[1] Most people would view it as simple common sense that the state has the right to give tax-funded contracts only to groups willing to provide the full range of services that the government deems desirable.

As I've noted, private businesses also fall under bright-line rules—even those that happen to be run by devoutly religious people. The mere fact that a corporation or a store is owned by a devout person does not free that person from complying with the nation's laws.

Most stores and businesses are considered public accommodations under the Civil Rights Act of 1964 and may not discriminate on the basis of race, gender, religion, or national origin. Sexual orientation is not yet protected by federal law but is in some states and localities. As laws extending civil-rights protections to members of the LGBTQ community grow, there will be conflicts when certain business owners cite their religious beliefs and refuse to provide services to gays.

I pointed out in the chapter on persecution that some cases like this have already occurred. Several concern people working in the wedding industry (caterers, photographers, bakers, etc.) who refuse to serve same-sex couples. Although fundamentalists may not like it, cultural trends are clearly breaking in favor of the expansion of gay rights, providing more opportunities for conflict.

These cases are bad enough. We take equal treatment seriously in America, and public-accommodation laws were long ago put in place to prevent invidious forms of discrimination. The injury is all the worse when it is coupled with a denial of desperately needed medical care.

A rape victim who can't get access to Plan B pills because the owner of a pharmacy cites religious freedom and refuses to hand them over is facing more than just an inconvenience. The law has the right (an obligation, actually) to address this issue, protect the victim, and see to her needs.

I would argue, in fact, for a broad legal principle that states that when medical needs and perceived slights to religious freedom come into conflict, it is the individual claiming the religious-liberty infringement who must meet a heightened standard of proof. The onus is on that person to prove beyond all doubt that the ability to exercise his or her religious-freedom rights somehow hinges on another person being denied medical rights. Admittedly, this will not be an easy standard to meet—nor should it be. We are talking about health matters here, perhaps literally issues dealing with life and death. In the face of this, it's not enough for someone to merely assert a religious-liberty right. There must be a standard of proof to meet—and it ought to be a high one.

In time, a legal answer will come from the courts, but the key to resolving these conflicts may rest with the culture. As tolerance of LGBTQ Americans expands, the country will eventually reach the point where open bigotry against gays is no longer socially acceptable, just as anti-Semitism and racial prejudice are today. (Of course, both still occur, but the law and the culture give them no harbor.)

Finally, we do have to face an unpleasant truth: much of these debates aren't about religious freedom; they are about power. Specifically, they are about power that has been lost. For a long time, conservative religious groups had the power to tell everyone else what to do. They ran our lives and often were able to employ the sword of the state when anyone resisted. It's still that way in some parts of the world, but people in the United States have tossed off that yoke.

Consider the hierarchy of the Catholic Church, which, for centuries, held sway over many Western nations. By banning birth control and abortion, they were able to control family life. Worse yet, they watched as their own flock ignored their teachings on this subject.

They lost that power.

Church leaders opposed divorce, so for a long time divorces were either next to impossible to get or flat-out illegal. Controlling divorce and having the ability to decide who could get one gave church fathers great power over families and communities.

They lost that power.

For a long time, the church's view of human sexuality held sway. The law punished people for perceived moral infractions or for engaging in certain types of sexual activities that church dogma labeled sinful—mainly homosexuality.

They lost that power.

The church enjoyed a long period where its sensibilities and theology determined what books people could read, what movies they could see, and what stage plays they could enjoy. This stranglehold over the culture helped ensure that people were exposed only to entertainment and messages that were first approved by church leaders.

They lost that power.

This string of losses has been difficult for ultraconservative church leaders to bear. To rationalize it, some have convinced themselves that the people really do agree with them but are being forced into a rigid box of secularization sponsored by the government.

Others have simply bided their time, waiting for any opportunity to get some of that old power back, to once again be in control. This spate of new claims of religious-freedom violations is really just a way to regain some lost ground. It's a power grab, dressed up in garb that ultraorthodox religious leaders hope we'll see as nonthreatening. "We're not trying to tell anyone what to do," they say, smiling. "We just want our religious freedom."

But at the end of the day, their interpretation of religious freedom would give them the right to tell others what to do. That's why their interpretation must be resisted.

Religious liberty (a principle that includes the right to reject religion entirely) is a treasured right of the American people. But it has never been interpreted as the right to impose your faith on others. The owner of a pharmacy may sincerely believe that birth control is a sin. Although strongly held, that belief gives him no right to impose this view on a woman seeking the medication her doctor has prescribed for her. Nor does it give a church the right to collect millions in tax dollars while acting as an agent for the state yet, at the same time, ignore the regulations that accompany said funding.

All religious groups have the right to spread their views and to try to persuade people to adopt them. All religious people have the right to meet for worship in fellowship with like-minded believers. All Americans have the right to support the religious groups of their choosing or to support none.

This is what religious freedom was meant to be. Somehow, that principle has been twisted to mean something else entirely—the right to tell other people what to do, or a so-called right to ignore any law that conflicts with whatever peculiar interpretation of faith one chooses to adopt.

Religious freedom has never meant this. It cannot mean this, not if we are to live together in mutual respect and peace.

No religious group has the right to use the government as the engine to propel its theology. The recent effort by some religious groups to define the concept of religious freedom to include a so-called right to rake in every dime of public funding available while remaining unaccountable to the taxpayers who provide that aid is offensive.

Nor do religious groups have a right to compel others to live under their rules, subject medical care to theology, or deny the civil rights of others because an interpretation of a book deemed holy has led a believer to adopt a certain position.

To adopt a theory of religious freedom that embraces these things does more than simply violate the rights of others. It makes a mockery of a great and noble principle.

NOTES

INTRODUCTION

1. *School Dist. of Abington Tp. v. Schempp*, 374 U.S. 203 (1963).

2. The quote appears in Jefferson's only published book, *Notes on the State of Virginia*, ed. Frank Shuffelton (New York: Penguin, 1998).

3. *United States v. Ogilvie*, No. 3:12-cr-00121-MMD-WGC, 2013 WL 1737243 (D. Nev. Apr. 22, 2013).

4. "Raw Milk Case against Amish Farmer Goes to Trial," Wisconsin Ag Connection, USAgNet.com, April 23, 2013, http://www.wisconsinag connection.com/story-state.php ?Id=484 (accessed November 6, 2013).

CHAPTER 1: HISTORY

1. Robert Boston, *Why the Religious Right Is Wrong about Separation of Church and State*, 2nd. ed. (Amherst, NY: Prometheus Books, 2003).

2. Glenn W. LaFantasie, ed., *The Correspondence of Roger Williams, Volume II: 1654–1682* (Providence, RI: Brown University Press, 1988), pp. 617–18.

3. Randall Balmer, Lee Groberg, and Mark Mabry, *First Freedom: The Fight for Religious Liberty* (American Fork, UT: Covenant Communications, 2012), p. 7.

4. "America's First Freedom: A Q&A with Religion Scholar Randall Balmer," *Church & State*, February 2013, pp. 13–15.

5. Isaac Backus, "An Appeal to the Public for Religious Liberty against the Oppressions of the Present Day," 1773, available online at http://classicliberal.tripod.com/misc/appeal.html (accessed November 19, 2013).

6. Joseph L. Conn, "Legacy of Liberty: Revolutionary-Era Pastor

John Leland Fought to Protect Religion from Government Interference," *Church & State*, October 2004, pp. 13–14.

7. Ibid.

8. Edwin S. Gaustad, *Sworn on the Altar of God: A Religious Biography of Thomas Jefferson* (Grand Rapids, MI: William B. Eerdmans, 1996), pp. 73–74.

9. Melvin I. Urofsky, *A Genesis of Religious Freedom: The Story of the Jews of Newport, RI and Touro Synagogue* (New York: George Washington Institute for Religious Freedom, 2013), p. 80.

10. Ibid.

11. Steven K. Green, *The Bible, the School, and the Constitution: The Clash That Shaped Modern Church-State Doctrine* (New York: Oxford University Press, 2012), pp. 137–77.

12. Warren Throckmorton and Michael Coulter, *Getting Jefferson Right: Fact-Checking Claims about Our Third President* (Grove City, PA: Salem Grove Press), ebook edition.

13. Boston, *Why the Religious Right Is Wrong*, pp. 264–66.

14. *Wisconsin v. Yoder*, 406 U.S. 205 (1972).

15. Sean Faircloth, *Attack of the Theocrats! How the Religious Right Harms Us All—and What We Can Do about It* (Charlottesville, VA: Pitchstone), pp. 56–57.

CHAPTER 2: RELIGION

1. "'Nones' on the Rise," Pew Research Center, Religion & Public Life Project, October 9, 21012, http://www.pewforum.org/2012/10/09/nones-on-the-rise/ (accessed November 13, 2013).

2. Robert Boston, *Why the Religious Right Is Wrong about Separation of Church and State*, 2nd ed. (Amherst, NY: Prometheus Books, 2003).

3. Robert S. Alley, *James Madison on Religious Liberty* (Amherst, NY: Prometheus Books, 1985), pp. 55–60.

4. Ibid.

5. "'Nones' on the Rise," Pew Research Center.

6. Rousas John Rushdoony, *The Institutes of Biblical Law* (Vallecito, CA: Craig Press, 1973), pp. 76–77.

7. See "Ground Zero Mosque," American Center for Law and Justice, http://aclj .org/ground-zero-mosque (accessed November 13, 2013).

8. Bob Smietana, "Legitimacy of Islam at Heart of Tenn. Mosque Suit," *USA Today*, October 4, 2010.

9. See "Confronting the Threat of Radical Islam," Thomas More Law Center, http://www.thomasmore.org/key-issues/confronting-the -threat-islam (accessed November 13, 2013).

10. Rob Boston, "Pentacle Quest Success!" *Church & State*, June 2007, pp. 4–7.

11. "Wiccan Priestess Wins Right to Perform Weddings in Va.— with AU's Help," *Church & State*, December 2012, p. 16.

CHAPTER 3: SEX

1. Rebecca Wind, "Premarital Sex Is Nearly Universal among Americans, and Has Been for Decades," Guttmacher Institute press release, December 19, 2006, http://www.guttmacher.org/media/nr/ 2006/12/19/index.html (accessed November 19, 2013).

2. *Griswold v. Connecticut*, 381 U.S. 479 (1965).

3. Ibid.

4. *Eisenstadt v. Baird*, 405 U.S. 438 (1972).

5. Katherine Mieszkowski, "Scientology's War on Psychiatry," *Salon*, July 1, 2005.

6. *Prince v. Massachusetts*, 321 U.S. 158 (1944).

7. *Sherbert v. Verner*, 374 U.S. 398 (1963).

8. "ACLU of Kentucky Statement on the Passage of HB279," American Civil Liberties Union of Kentucky press release, March 11, 2013, https://www.aclu.org/lgbt-rights-racial-justice-religion-belief -womens-rights/aclu-kentucky-statement-passage-hb279 (accessed November 19, 2013).

9. Ellen Goodman, "The Truth about Teens and Sex," *Boston Globe*, January 3, 2009.

10. Rob Stein, "Premarital Abstinence Pledges Ineffective, Study Finds," *Washington Post*, December 29, 2008.

11. *Hollingsworth v. Perry*, 12-144 (2013), brief Amicus Curiae of

United States Conference of Catholic Bishops in Support of Petitioners and Supporting Reversal, p. 24.

12. Jon Cohen, "Gay Marriage Support Hits New High in Post-ABC Poll," *Washington Post*, March 18, 2013.

13. Bryan Fischer, *Focal Point*, American Family Radio, March 18, 2013.

CHAPTER 4: EDUCATION

1. Boardman W. Kathan, "Prayer and the Public Schools: The Issue in Historical Perspective and Implications for Religious Education Today," *Religious Education* 84, no. 2 (spring 1981): 232–48.

2. *Board of Education of Cincinnati v. Minor*, 23 Ohio St. 211 (1872).

3. Michael Feldberg, *The Philadelphia Riots of 1844: A Study of Ethnic Conflict* (Westport, CT: Greenwood Press, 1975).

4. *Edwards v. Aguillard*, 482 U.S. 578 (1987).

5. *Kitzmiller v. Dover Area School District*, 400 F. Supp. 2d 707 (2005).

6. Christine Garwood, *Flat Earth: The History of an Infamous Idea* (New York: Thomas Dunne Books, 2008), pp. 210–11.

7. "Credo of the Biblical Astronomer," Geocentricity.com, www.geo centricity.com/bibastron/credo.html (accessed November 25, 2013).

8. *Pierce v. Society of Sisters*, 268 U.S. 510 (1925).

CHAPTER 5: POLITICS

1. Laura Strickler, "Senate Panel Probes 6 Top Televangelists," *CBS News*, November 6, 2007, http://www.cbsnews.com/2100-500690_162 -3456977.html (accessed November 25, 2013).

2. *Branch Ministries v. Rosotti*, 211 F.3d 137 (2000).

3. Joseph L. Conn, "Tax-Exempt Electioneering? Gay-Bashing Pastor's Obama Animus Crosses IRS Line," *Church & State*, July–August 2012, pp. 13–14. All spellings in this quote are retained from the original source material.

4. Ibid.

5. "Full Text of Bishop Jenky's Homily at Men's March and Mass," *Catholic Post*, http://www.thecatholicpost.com/post/PostArticle.aspx?ID=2440 (accessed December 5, 2013).

6. Ibid.

7. Dennis Coday, "Peoria Bishop Orders Catholics to the Polls," *National Catholic Reporter Online*, October 31, 2012, ncronline.org/blogs/ncr-today/peoria-bishop-orders-catholics-polls (accessed November 26, 2013).

8. "Bishop Ricken: Voting for Candidate Who Favors Intrinsic Evils 'Could Put Your Own Soul in Jeopardy,'" CatholicCulture.org, Catholic World News, October 29, 2012, www.catholicculture.org/news/headlines/index.cfm?storyid=16066 (accessed November 26, 2013).

9. *Walz v. Tax Commission of the City of New York*, 397 U.S. 664 (1970).

10. José Maria Eça de Queirós, *The Maias* (New York: New Directions, 2007).

11. *Hollingsworth v. Perry*, 12-144 (2013), brief Amicus Curiae of United States Conference of Catholic Bishops in Support of Petitioners and Supporting Reversal, p. 24.

CHAPTER 6: CULTURE

1. Jacqueline Trescott, "Transformer Shows Banned Video, as Debate over Museum's Censorship Rages," *Washington Post*, December 2, 2010.

2. Jacqueline Trescott, "Ant-Covered Jesus Video Removed from Smithsonian after Catholic League Complains," *Washington Post*, December 1, 2010.

3. Sabrina Tavernise, "Smithsonian Official Defends Disputed Video's Exhibit," *New York Times*, January 31, 2011.

4. Froma Harrop, "Kerik Fiasco Splatters More Mud on Giuliani," *Seattle Times*, December 16, 2004.

5. Rob Boston, "The Art of Censorship: Catholic League, Congressional Allies Push 'Sacrilegious' Video from National Portrait Gallery," *Church & State*, January 2011, pp. 4–6.

6. Bill Berkowitz, "Catholic League's William Donohue's Rage against the Jews," *Talk to Action* (blog), June 27, 2012, http://www

.talk2action.org/story/2012/6/27/115918/088/Dominionism_in_the
_military/Catholic_League_s_William_Donohue_s_Rage_Against_the
_Jews (accessed November 26, 2013).

7. Paul Blanshard, *American Freedom and Catholic Power* (Boston: Beacon Press, 1951), p. 199.

8. Paul Blanshard, *The Right to Read* (Boston: Beacon Press, 1955).

9. *Joseph Burstyn, Inc. v. Wilson*, 343 U.S. 495 (1952).

10. *Mutual Film Corporation v. Industrial Commission of Ohio*, 236 U.S. 230 (1915).

11. Thomas Lindlof, *Hollywood under Siege: Martin Scorsese, the Religious Right, and the Culture Wars* (Lexington: University Press of Kentucky, 2008).

12. H. L. Mencken, *A Mencken Chrestomathy* (New York: Knopf, 1949).

13. "History of Rock and Roll: Major Influence Chart," *Christian News*, December 14, 1987, p. 9.

14. J. Royce Thomason, "Strange Effects of Music," *Christian News*, December 14, 1987, p. 9.

CHAPTER 7: PERSECUTION

1. Lobby Disclosure Act of 1995, Pub. L. No. 104–65, 104th Cong., 109 Stat. 691, § III, 8B (1995).

2. *Goodridge v. Dept. of Public Health*, 798 N.E. 2d 941 (Mass. 2003).

3. Gary Langer, "Poll Tracks Dramatic Rise in Support for Gay Marriage," ABC News, March 18, 2013.

4. Meredith Bennett-Smith, "Janet Mefferd, Conservative Host, Says Anti-Gay Activists Will Be Treated Like 'Jews in Nazi Germany,'" *Huffington Post*, April 12, 2013, http://www.huffingtonpost.com/ 2013/04/12/janet-mefferd-anti-gay-activists-jews-nazi-germany_n _3063714.html (accessed November 26, 2013).

5. Brian Tashman, "Perkins: 'Revolution' Possible If 'Court Goes Too Far' on Marriage Equality Cases," *Right-Wing Watch*, March 26, 2013, http://www.rightwingwatch.org/content/perkins-revolution-possible -if-court-goes-too-far-marriage-equality-cases#sthash.AWGaXn4k .dpuf (accessed November 26, 2013).

6. Rob Boston, "An Invitation to Tea: 'Values Voter' Summiteers

Seek Marriage of Convenience with Tea Party Activists in Advance of November Elections," *Church & State*, October 2010, p. 9.

7. The phrase appears on the website of the Blackstone Legal Fellowship, a program to train attorneys, which is described as a "ministry of the Alliance Defending Freedom." See http://www.blackstone legalfellowship.org/Resources/ResourceOverview (accessed November 27, 2013).

CONCLUSION: RUN YOUR OWN LIFE, NOT MINE

1. Stephanie Mencimer, "Rep. Darrell Issa Comes out Swinging for Catholic Bishops," *Mother Jones*, December 2, 2011.

SELECT BIBLIOGRAPHY

Allen, Brooke. *Moral Minority: Our Skeptical Founding Fathers.* Chicago: Ivan R. Dee, 2006.

Alley, Robert S. *James Madison on Religious Liberty.* Amherst, NY: Prometheus Books, 1985.

Austin, Michael. *That's Not What They Meant! Reclaiming the Founding Fathers from America's Right Wing.* Amherst, NY: Prometheus Books, 2012.

Balmer, Randall. *First Freedom: The Fight for Religious Liberty.* American Fork, UT: Covenant Communications, 2012.

Barry, John M. *Roger Williams and the Creation of the American Soul: Church, State and the Birth of Liberty.* New York: Penguin Books, 2012.

Blaker, Kimberly, ed. *The Fundamentals of Extremism: The Christian Right in America.* New Boston, MI: New Boston Books, 2003.

Bracey, Gerald W. *Setting the Record Straight: Responses to Misconceptions about Public Education in the United States.* Alexandria, VA: Association for Supervision and Curriculum Development, 1997.

Buckner, Edward M., and Michael E. Buckner. *In Freedom We Trust: An Atheist Guide to Religious Liberty.* Amherst, NY: Prometheus Books, 2012.

Dierenfield, Bruce J. *The Battle over School Prayer: How* Engel v. Vitale *Changed America.* Lawrence: University Press of Kansas, 2007.

Faircloth, Sean. *Attack of the Theocrats! How the Religious Right Harms Us All—And What We Can Do about It.* Charlottesville, VA: Pitchstone Publishing, 2012.

Gaddy, C. Welton, and Barry W. Lynn. *First Freedom First: A Citizens' Guide to Protecting Religious Liberty and the Separation of Church and State.* Boston: Beacon Press, 2008.

Gaustad, Edwin S. *Sworn on the Altar of God: A Religious Biography of Thomas Jefferson.* Grand Rapids, MI: William B. Eerdmans, 1996.

Green, Steven K. *The Bible, the School and the Constitution: The Clash That Shaped Modern Church-State Doctrine.* New York: Oxford University Press, 2012.

Hamilton, Marci A. *God vs. the Gavel: Religion and the Rule of Law.* Cambridge: Cambridge University Press, 2005.

Jacoby, Susan. *Freethinkers: A History of American Secularism.* New York: Metropolitan Books, 2004.

Jefferson, Thomas. *The Jefferson Bible: The Life and Morals of Jesus of Nazareth Extracted Textually from the Gospels in Greek, Latin, French & English.* Washington, DC: Smithsonian Books, 2011.

Kramnick, Isaac, and R. Laurence Moore. *The Godless Constitution: The Case against Religious Correctness.* New York: W. W. Norton, 1997.

Lambert, Frank. *The Founding Fathers and the Place of Religion in America.* Princeton, NJ: Princeton University Press, 2003.

Lebo, Lauri. *The Devil in Dover: An Insider's Story of Dogma v. Darwin in Small-Town America.* New York: New Press, 2008.

Lynn, Barry W. *Piety & Politics: The Right-Wing Assault on Religious Freedom.* New York: Harmony, 2006.

Niose, David. *Nonbeliever Nation: The Rise of Secular Americans.* New York: Palgrave Macmillan, 2012.

Padover, Saul K., ed. *Thomas Jefferson on Democracy.* New York: Mentor Books, 1958.

Phillips, Kevin: *American Theocracy: The Peril and Politics of Radical Religion, Oil, and Borrowed Money in the 21st Century.* New York: Viking, 2006.

Posner, Sarah. *God's Profits: Faith, Fraud, and the Republican Crusade for Values Voters.* Sausalito, CA: PoliPoint Press, 2008.

Rodda, Chris. *Liars for Jesus: The Religious Right's Alternate Version of American History.* Volume 1. [NJ]: Chris Rodda, 2006.

Solomon, Stephen D. *Ellery's Protest: How One Young Man Defied Tradition and Sparked the Battle over School Prayer.* Ann Arbor: University of Michigan Press, 2007.

Stewart, Katherine. *The Good News Club: The Christian Right's Stealth Assault on America's Children.* New York: PublicAffairs Books, 2012.

Throckmorton, Warren, and Michael Coulter. *Getting Jefferson Right: Fact Checking Claims about Our Third President.* Grove City, PA: Salem Grove Press, 2012.

Whitten, Mark Weldon. *The Myth of Christian America: What You Need to Know about the Separation of Church and State.* Macon, GA: Smith and Helwys, 1999.

INDEX